D0638672

THOMAS MERTON
Preview of the Asian Journey

THOMAS MERTON

Preview of the Asian Journey

Edited, with an introduction, by
WALTER H. CAPPS

CROSSROAD · NEW YORK

1989
The Crossroad Publishing Company
370 Lexington Avenue, New York, N.Y. 10017

Printed in the United States of America

Library of Congress Cataloging-in-Publication Data

Merton, Thomas, 1915–1968.
    Thomas Merton : preview of the Asian journey / edited with an
introduction by Walter H. Capps.
        p. cm.
    Bibliography: p.
    ISBN 0-8245-0951-X
    1. Monastic and religious life. 2. East and West. 3. Merton,
Thomas, 1915–1968—Interviews.   I. Capps, Walter H. II. Title.
BX2435.M48   1989
255—dc20   89-32636
                                                              CIP

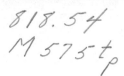
for Eulah Laucks

CONTENTS

THOMAS MERTON
Preview of the Asian Journey

INTRODUCTION

On October 3, 1968, just days before embarking on his fateful journey to Asia, Thomas Merton, the famous Trappist monk, came to Santa Barbara, California, to make a brief informal presentation before a meeting of the Center for the Study of Democratic Institutions. The center had been established by Robert Hutchins, and his colleagues and associates, in 1959, as a place where the major issues of the day would be addressed in depth, with the intention of anticipating the needs and vulnerabilities of the democratic society. Merton had been persuaded to submit some of his views to this forum by W. H. "Ping" Ferry, a senior fellow at the center, and a friend of Merton, who had been corresponding with the monk for a number of years.

It was the practice at the center to record and transcribe the discussions of the dialogue sessions for the files. Several paragraphs of Merton's comments on the nature of the monastic life were

1

subsequently transcribed, edited, and published in a brief article in the *Center Magazine*. But not until now has the transcript of the entire conversation been made available. We are publishing it on the twentieth anniversary of Merton's visit to Santa Barbara and, thus, on the twentieth anniversary of his death. Needless to say, the entire discussion carries a relevance now that wasn't and couldn't have been recognized at the time.

The recorded conversation is important for several reasons. First, Merton's travels outside the Abbey of Our Lady of Gethsemani were rather few. He did visit other monasteries belonging to the Trappists within the United States and made frequent visits to nearby Louisville on errands, or to discuss aspects of his literary work. But the journey to the West Coast (to Alaska and California), before proceeding to Asia, was his first extended time away from the monastic community after taking his initial vows some twenty-seven years before. What does a monk choose to do the first time he is away from his abbey? What does he talk about? How does he describe his vocation to those who are not fully familiar? What assessment of the monastic way of life does he offer when called upon to offer description and interpretation? There is curiosity about these questions regardless of who the monk might be. But when the monk in question is, perhaps, the most well-known monk of all, the questions become very much more significant.

Second, to my knowledge this was the only time, since joining the order, that Merton appeared before a gathering of intellectuals (only some of which would have accepted his principal assumptions) to share and test his ideas. Monks are not often brought into such gatherings, and they certainly do not seek them out. Merton hadn't been involved in anything quite like this since leaving Columbia University as a graduate student. The record of what he said on this occasion, and how he responded to comments and criticism, offers an illustration of the way in which he operated in dialogical and dialectical situations. Here was an opportunity to test his ideas and sensibilities within the context of a very lively intellectual forum. Few gathered there would have deferred to him because of the sanctity of his vocation. No one found him daunting simply because he was already the well-known author of a significant number of books. On the contrary, he was approached and treated as anyone else would be who had ideas and proposals to share. Fortunately, for our purposes, the entire conversation was recorded and transcribed. We have provided an edited version in the pages that follow. It is an account of a significant event that occurred that day.

Third, Merton's stopover in Santa Barbara occurred only a week and a half before he left San Francisco on his way to Asia, a journey from which he did not return. From the first he had understood his travel to the Orient to be a pilgrimage, and was full of excitement and anticipation concerning what he would find there. In preparation for his trip, he had been immersing himself in the writings of the Asian religious traditions. He had been reading Clifford Geertz's anthropological analyses of Javanese culture. He had been trying to acquaint himself with the spiritual teachings of Tibetan Buddhism as preparation for a hoped-for meeting with the Dalai Lama. He had been continuing his study of Zen, and had just published *Zen and the Birds of Appetite*.[1] In a multitude of ways, he had been trying to sensitize himself to receive the wisdom of Asian monasticism. He had believed that Asian monks were far ahead of their Western counterparts in some aspects of the monastic vocation. Thus, he had come to view his journey to Asia as providing the next essential steps in his own spiritual pilgrimage. He knew that it would be decisive, and he wanted to be ready when the opportunity came. Therefore, what he was thinking about just days before he left the country, and the terms under which he was anticipating the encounter, are unusually significant. They give some hint of what his journey was about, what he expected to learn, what he anticipated being able to accomplish, and the purposes it would serve if the encounter lived up to his anticipations.

As noted, Thomas Merton's appearance at the Center for the Study of Democratic Institutions had been arranged by W. H. "Ping" Ferry, vice-president of the organization at the time, who had been corresponding with the Trappist monk since 1961. Merton had become acquainted with the work of the center, had read many of its publications, and had offered his services, in whatever ways might be appropriate, to Robert Hutchins and his colleagues. In his first letter to Ferry, Merton proposed that "a contemplative monk should have a quiet though articulate place in the discussions of his time."[2] He also suggested that there is a "contemplative approach to the present world situation." And he believed that it ought to become a deliberate and articulable ingredient in the center's work.

Through the years, Ferry and Merton exchanged notes about books and articles. Ferry sent materials to Merton, and Merton began sending mimeographed copies of his own essays to Ferry, and sought his appraisal as well as his advice as to how and where items might be published. And as the mail flowed in both directions, so were ideas generated. In effect, the two created a dialogue by correspondence.

Soon Ferry was to visit Merton at Gethsemani and then returned on several occasions. When Merton was hospitalized for surgery in 1966 and developed what he called "a deep relationship" with one of the nurses who had been caring for him, he asked his friend Ping Ferry to come to Louisville so that he could talk about it. On occasion, Ferry sent visitors Merton's way. Following such visits, the two of them would exchange correspondence concerning their impressions.

Domestic life changed for Thomas Merton when a new abbot was appointed at Gethsemani, an abbot who gave him permission to travel. In May 1968, Merton left the abbey to journey to Our Lady of the Redwoods Abbey, the Trappistine center, in northern California. On this trip he spent a day in San Francisco, where he saw the poet Lawrence Ferlinghetti, and where he also met Ferry. Then Merton went to the Monastery of Christ in the Desert in Abiquiu, New Mexico, before returning to Gethsemani.

In June 1968, Merton wrote Ferry about desiring a return visit to the West Coast. By now he was deeply interested in relocating and was contemplating the possibility of establishing a hermitage for himself somewhere in the western portion of the United States, most probably in California, but perhaps in Alaska. He wrote Ferry, "I am fully set on spending any time I can on that shore, and wish I could move out for keeps."

In July he was working on a specific itinerary, and he wrote Ferry about places he wanted to visit on the California coast. Ferry promised to escort him.

By early September Merton's itinerary was in place, and he notified his Santa Barbara friend that he would fly to New Mexico, then to Alaska, then to Santa Barbara. On September 25, he wrote Ferry from Anchorage that he would arrive in Santa Barbara on October 3. He agreed to make a presentation to the center so long, as he put it, as there was "no immediate press publicity." He said that he would "present some informal ideas as to how everything looks about the trip [his Asian journey] now." He proposed that this presentation be the first in a two-part series. When returning from Asia, he would report on what he had learned, whether his expectations had been fulfilled, and so forth. He called it "before and after, so to speak," and offered that "it could be quite interesting." The plan, following the presentation at the center, was for Ferry to accompany Merton on a drive along the California coast, where the two of them could survey possible hermitage locations. Merton was also going to check in with the sisters at the Redwoods abbey near Whitethorn and then leave for Asia. This happened, not altogether on schedule, but Ping Ferry was present when Thomas Merton left San Francisco, having taken him to the airport.[3]

We already know something of the subject that preoccupied him because we have the diary that Merton kept while en route, namely, his unfinished *Asian Journal*. Because of its incomplete and prophetic—and thus provocative and enigmatic—character, the *Asian Journal*[4] will stand for Merton's era as Dietrich Bonhoeffer's *Letters and Papers from Prison*[5] does for his. The document provides a powerfully lucid anticipatory look into the religious future on the part of someone who is in process of journeying there, being attentive, all the while, to what he is experiencing. Neither Merton nor Bonhoeffer lived to see the dawning of the future each had anticipated, but they would have recognized it if they had, and they did identify many of its distinguishing configurations in advance. The *Asian Journal* is not only a transitional piece; in some respects, it is also epoch-making. It offers a look into a future that regards the religious traditions of the world to be in effective reciprocal relationship with each other. In addition, it provides strong clues regarding demonstrative ways in which Christians might approach or meet or engage Asian religious traditions and view them as enhancements instead of threats or competitors to the faith.

And the fourth reason for the significance of the conversation pertains to the access it offers to the manner and style according to which Thomas Merton thought and spoke. Through his many essays and books, the late Trappist has left a large legacy of examples that illustrate the way in which his mind worked when his task was to write his thoughts and ideas on paper. And we have rich and numerous examples of the ways in which such thoughts were set down when he wrote letters to friends, colleagues, well-wishers, and inquirers. But there are only scant records of Merton talking, and none, to my knowledge, of Merton engaged in conversation with persons outside professional religious communities. The discussion we have recorded and transcribed illustrates the ways in which he worked and proceeded within this context. It shows his intellectual seriousness. It reveals his remarkable wit as well as his tendency to be self-deprecating. It discloses his disposition to be critical of some of the institutional features of the way of life to which he had committed himself. And it gives evidence of his willingness to be sharply critical of some of the prevailing attitudes and practices of the Catholic Church. But, most impressively of all, the transcript of the conversation gives evidence of Merton's unusual ability to exercise control over the multidimensionality of such conversations.

Theologically and intellectually speaking, he had been advancing his viewpoint toward the Asian religions as early as 1963 in his essay "A Letter to Pablo Antonio Caudra Concerning Giants," which was published in his *Emblems of a Season of Fury*. Here, in describing typically Western attitudes to cultures and traditions not Western, he had decried "the unmitigated arrogance [of the West] towards the rest of the human race."[6] He suggested that if Western Christians are to take the doctrine of the incarnation seriously, they will find God present in all persons, regardless of their race, culture, or geographical location. Citing the verse from Matthew in which Jesus Christ says, "I was thirsty and you gave me not to drink. I was hungry and you gave me not to eat," Merton comments:

> This could be extended in every possible sense: and is meant to be so extended, all over the entire area of human needs, not only for bread, for work, for liberty, for health, but also for truth, for belief, for love, for acceptance, for fellowship and understanding.[7]

Then he suggests that it was "one of the great tragedies of the West" that the missionaries, for all of their good will and noble intentions, did and "could not recognize that the races they conquered were essentially equal to themselves and in some ways superior." He talks of the conjunction of Christianity with Roman and Greek cultures as having made impressive historical and philosophical sense, but not as being normative for everyone. So too with the conjunction of Christianity with Jewish life and culture. The principle is that the Christian religion "made its way in the world of the first century not by imposing Jewish cultural and social standards on the rest of the world, but by abandoning them, getting free of them so as to be 'all things to all men.' " There are several sides to this assertion. First, as he put it, Christ "is found less in a truth that is imposed than in a truth that is shared."[8] Second, also in his own words, "God is to be heard, not only on Sinai, not only in my own heart, but in the voice of the stranger."[9] And this leads to a discussion of Christian missionary activity in both China and India. Merton believed that India and China each had and have a lot to say to the Christian West, but each one's message has been muted. The same is true, as well, of the voice of Latin America. Merton chides: "If I insist on giving you my truth, and never stop to receive your truth in return, then there can be no truth between us."[10] This is followed by an extended passage that reflects Merton's views on the relationships between Christianity and other religious traditions:

> Christ is present "where two or three are gathered in my name." But to be gathered in the name of Christ is to be gathered in the name of the Word made flesh, of God made man. It is therefore to be gathered in the faith that God has become man and can be seen in man, that he can speak in man and that he can enlighten and inspire love in and through any man I meet."[11]

And this provides motivation for missionary work:

> It is true that the visible Church alone has the official mission to sanctify and teach all nations, but no man knows that the stranger he meets coming out of the forest in a new country is not already an invisible member of Christ and perhaps one who has some providential message to utter.[12]

This is followed by a vivid image:

> So the tourist drinks tequila, and thinks it is no
> good, and waits for the fiesta he has been told
> to wait for. How should he realize that the
> Indian who walks down the street with half a
> house on his head and a hole in his pants, is
> Christ? All the tourist thinks is that it is odd for
> so many Indians to be called Jesus.[13]

The essays included in *Mystics and Zen Masters*
follow similar pathways of development.[14] Here
Merton's purpose is to interpret the points of view
of Zen Buddhism, oriental mysticism, classical
Chinese thought, Taoism, and the principles of
Buddhist monasticism accurately and vividly. His
desire is to describe the perceptions of reality that
prevail within these orientations, and he is conscious that he is writing for Westerners for whom
such portrayals may serve as the first encounter
with the religions of Asia. But he can hardly
achieve these purposes without disclosing his own
attitude to those religions and specifying ways in
which Christians might appropriately approach or
engage them. For this, he follows the principle
enunciated at the Second Vatican Council, namely,
that "the Catholic Church rejects nothing which is
true and holy in these religions," affirming that
they "often reflect a ray of that Truth which en-
lightens all men."[15] Merton comments that this is
the spirit he is invoking, too, when describing the

intentions and achievements of Asian religions. He indicates that it wouldn't suffice for him "to look at these other traditions coldly and objectively from the outside, but, in some measure at least, to try to share in the values and the experience which they embody."[16] In explaining this intention, he acknowledges that he is "not content to write about them without making them, as far as possible, 'his own.' "[17] It is clear, from all of this, that Merton did not approach the religions of Asia as being competitors of Christianity, or even as rivals for the truth. On the contrary, his disposition was to approach them as being compatible with Christian beliefs and practice, as if each might assist the other in coming to a fullness of insight and knowedge. It is clear, too, that Merton understood his own engagement with Asian spiritual pathways to be necessary to his own maturation both as a Christian and as a human being. And what he understood to be necessary for himself he also understood to be necessary for the world.[18] If the world was to come to the kind of global understanding that might diminish the prospects of a nuclear holocaust, it was essential that Westerners overcome their own arrogance toward non-Westerners and begin to recognize the wisdom of the East and its applicability to deeply perceived human spiritual need.

This is the same vantage point that prevails, with extensions and amendations, in the book *Zen and the Birds of Appetite*. This was the study that was to take him even deeper into an understanding of Zen, which he had consistently been describing as something other than dogma or theology or abstract metaphysical truth. He had been referring to it, instead, at least from *Mystics and Zen Masters* on, as "a concrete and lived ontology which explains itself not in theoretical propositions, but in acts emerging out of a certain quality of consciousness and of awareness."[19] Thus, the intention of *Zen and the Birds of Appetite* was to probe that "lived ontology" further.

Zen and the Birds of Appetite constitutes some of Merton's most perceptive thinking and clearest writing. In my judgment, it shows him at his best—yes—at the top of his form. His intention was to come to terms with Zen philosophy, in contrast or relationship to the dominant or prevailing ways of thinking and being in the Western world. It represented a major challenge for him because he knew that Zen understanding can only transpire via a negation of the standard or typical ways of analysis and comprehension that have grown up in the West. And yet he also recognized that he already knew something implicitly about Zen simply on the basis of a portion of his experience as a monk and a hermit. The latter experience stimulated a sense of readiness or preparedness for Zen, albeit a preparedness that is aware of the fact that it relates by contrast and negation. As he puts it:

To define Zen in terms of a religious system or structure is in fact to destroy it—or rather to miss it completely, for what cannot be "constructed" cannot be destroyed either. Zen is not something which is grasped by being set within distinct limits or given a characteristic outline or easily recognizable features so that, when we see these distinct and particular forms, we say: "There it is!" Zen is not understood by being set apart in its own category, separated from everything else: "It is *this* and not *that*." On the contrary, in the words of D. T. Suzuki, Zen is "beyond the world of opposites, a world built up by intellectual distinction . . . a spiritual world of nondistinction which involves achieving an absolute point of view."[20]

Merton concludes from Suzuki's words that:

Zen is outside all particular structures and distinct forms, and that it is neither opposed to them or not-opposed to them. It neither denies them nor affirms them, loves them nor hates them, rejects them nor desires them. Zen is consciousness unstructured by particular form or particular system, a trans-cultural, trans-religious, trans-formed consciousness. It is therefore in a sense "void." But it can shine through this or that system, religious or irreligious, just as light can shine through glass that is blue, or green, or red, or yellow. If Zen has any preference it is for glass that is plain, has no color, and is "just glass."[21]

This leads him to inquire into the basis of the Christian religion, which, before he is finished, takes him into the writings of Meister Eckhart, because of the latter's emphasis upon *kenosis,* or the identification of that which is essentially Christian with St. Paul's description of the "self-emptying" of Jesus Christ. Merton is fascinated by Eckhart's "Zen-like equation of God as infinite abyss and ground," and quotes Eckhart's description of "perfect poverty" as follows:

> Man's last and highest parting occurs when for God's sake he takes leave of god. St. Paul took leave of god for God's sake and gave up all that he might get from god as well as all he might give—together with every idea of god. In parting with these he parted with god for God's sake and God remained in him as God is in his own nature—not as he is conceived by anyone to be—nor yet as something yet to be achieved, but more as an is-ness, as God really is. Then he and God were a unit, that is pure unity. Thus one becomes that real person for whom there can be no suffering, any more than the divine essence can suffer.[22]

Given differences in cultural experiences and modes of communication, Merton believes that some of Eckhart's descriptions are "very close to the expressions we find everywhere in the Zen Masters." He is attracted to Eckhart's identification of one's true identity with "the birth of Christ in us," which birth carries significant resemblances to the way in which Suzuki and other Zen authors write. Merton elaborates:

> Curiously, then, for Eckhart, it is when we lose our special, separate cultural and religious identity—the "self" or "persona" that is the subject of virtues as well as visions, that perfects itself by good works, that advances in the practice of piety—that Christ is finally born in us in the highest sense.[23]

He understands why Eckhart's teachings were disturbing. Any philosophy that counseled losing or abandoning one's "separate cultural and religious identity" would be, particularly if this is construed as recommending an identity that even transcends identification with the Christian religion. He explains it this way:

> In all that he tried to say, whether in familiar or in startling terms, Eckhart was trying to point to something that cannot be structured and cannot be contained within the limits of any system. He was not trying to construct a new dogmatic theology, but was trying to give expression to the great creative renewal of the mystical consciousness which was sweeping through the Rhineland and the Low Countries in his time. . . . Seen in relation to those Zen

Masters on the other side of the earth who, like him, deliberately used extremely paradoxical expressions, we can detect in him the same kind of consciousness as theirs.[24]

Then comes the shift back to a fresh consideration of Zen:

Whatever Zen may be, however you define it, it is somehow there in Eckhart. But the way to see it is not first to define Zen and then apply the definition both to him and to the Japanese Zen Masters. The real way to study Zen is to penetrate the outer shell and taste the inner kernel which cannot be defined. Then one realizes in oneself the reality which is being talked about.[25]

Merton also devotes *Zen and the Birds of Appetite* to a description of the shifts in religious and spiritual consciousness that he understood to be occurring in the Western world. He is sharply critical of the postconciliar emphasis upon "activistic, secular and antimystical" Christianity." His reference point, if now by contrast, is the Western religious consciousness that "remained more or less the same from Augustine to Maritain." He recognizes that modern Christian consciousness cannot be identical to the faith of first-century Christians. Rather, modern Christian consciousness "is bound to be a modern consciousness." But if modern, then how is it still affected by the philosophy of Descartes, for whom self-awareness ("as a thinking, observing, measuring and estimating 'self'") is "absolutely primary?" Merton believes the Christian challenge requires a transcending of the limits of the Cartesian sensibility, which approaches the ego, or the self, as being "imprisoned in its own consciousness, isolated and out of touch with other such selves in so far as they are all 'things' rather than persons."[26] Merton attests that persons of religious sensitivity in the Western world are searching for effective alternatives to the Cartesian obstructions. Indeed, there is evidence of the desire for liberation from such "inordinate self-consciousness," which Merton also describes as "monumental self-awareness" as well as "obsessions with self-affirmation." At the same time, modern consciousness does not find previous Hellenic thought categories to carry much vitality and no longer draws intellectual or spiritual vitality out of Platonic dualisms. Where to go and what to do now that the inadequacies of such spiritual orientations have become self-evident? Merton offers that Christians "will do well to return to the simple lessons of the Gospel," which lessons can be understood not through cultural experience "that thrives on the stimulation and exploitation of egocentric desire," but through "unworldliness," which he describes as "the basic teaching of Buddhism." The good news of redemption is the experience of a liberation that is both "life-affirming" and "life-denying." He describes it as a "freedom . . . that goes with being simply what [one] is and accepting things as they are in order to work with them as [one] can."[27] Merton understands this to be coming to terms with that which is absolutely essential.

All of this was in his mind when he recognized the need to do more than simply study the texts, talk to expert witnesses, and write descriptive and interpretive essays. It was necessary for him to travel, to undertake a pilgrimage to Asia, so that he could make his own observations within the natural habitat of the Asian religious traditions he had only envisioned from afar. He wanted to be able to witness them in their own terms, on their own grounds, and within the cultures they had influenced and inspired, and to which they had lent most significant formation. He wanted to travel because this pilgrimage represented the next stage in the development of his own spiritual path. He was excited by the prospect that would soon be his. To enable himself to take the fullest advantage of it when it came, he had been preparing himself both spiritually and intellectually. He had been reading the commentaries, the critical literature, and the textual interpretations which he knew to be the most reliable; and he had been testing some hypotheses, in advance, before he would have the opportunity to examine the evidence at close range. He came to Santa Barbara ready for the journey.

And those at the Center for the Study of Democratic Institutions who understood something of what he was about were eager to put questions to him, eager to find out what it was that was drawing him to Asia, but, perhaps, more eager to learn more about just who he was. His reputation had preceded him, of course, for Thomas Merton as the author of numerous books was well known. But the conversation with the fellows of the center would provide an opportunity for him to present himself, as well as his views, in a new and fresh way. And it would create the occasion within which there could be some significant intellectual give-and-take—a situation that many authors, particularly those who live as monastic hermits, cannot always avail themselves of.

We have transcribed the conversation (editing it only lightly) in virtually verbatim form. Merton begins with a reference to his book *Zen and the Birds of Appetite* because Ferry, his friend, had referred to it when making the introduction. In obvious narrative fashion, Merton next proceeds to explain why he is in Santa Barbara, and this gives him the opportunity to talk about his upcoming trip to Asia and what he expects to see, discover, and encounter there. His discussion at this point encourages those around the dialogue table to focus on the relationships between the two cultures and the relationships between Western and non-

Western religious traditions. While on this subject, Merton offers some commentary on Javanese religion—he had been reading rather heavily on this subject—and talks of anticipating meeting the Dalai Lama. As he talks, his listeners are thinking of contrasts between East and West, between Asian religions and what they know of developments within contemporary Western (primarily American) Christianity. This forces Merton—because the question is put directly to him—to provide some commentary on the strengths and weaknesses of the Christian religion, or, more specifically, the Catholic Church. And he obliges; he is very critical indeed of certain aspects of contemporary Catholicism. He is similarly critical of some of the more formal characteristics of Christian monasticism. And he wonders out loud how either or both might be reformed, and at what degree of cost to the institutions involved.

The transcript of the discussion provides illumination of some of the topics Merton would continue to address as he journeyed in Asia. Clearly, he had hopes for the pilgrimage and much respect for its providential quality. It culminated, as the world now knows, in his meeting with the Dalai Lama on November 4, and then, a month later, on December 1, with his encounter with the Buddhist sculptures at Polonnaruwa. It was here that his Asian experience had come to clarity, as he wrote in his journal:

Looking at these figures, I was suddenly, almost forcibly, jerked clean out of the habitual, half-tied vision of things, and an inner clearness, clarity, as if exploding from the rocks themselves, became evident and obvious.

He added:

I don't know when in my life I have ever had such a sense of beauty and spiritual validity running together in one aesthetic illumination.

And he concluded:

Surely, with Hamabalipuram and Polonnaruwa my Asian pilgrimage has become clear and purified itself. I mean, I know and have seen what I was obscurely looking for. I don't know what else remains but I have now seen and have pierced through the surface and have got beyond the shadow and the disguise. This is Asia in its purity, not covered over with garbage, Asian or European or American, and it is clear, pure, complete. It says everything; it needs nothing. And because it needs nothing it can afford to be silent, unnoticed, undiscovered. It does not need to be discovered. It is we, Asians included, who need to discover it.[28]

Years later, when I asked Father Jean Leclercq, Merton's friend and colleague, what he understood the passage to mean, I received this response: "Merton saw what was there, and he understood that he was seeing it as it truly is."[29]

As the world now also knows, Thomas Merton lived only a week and a half more. He died in Bangkok on December 10 and was buried in a simple grave, according to long-standing Cistercian tradition, on the grounds of the abbey in Kentucky on the afternoon of December 17. But, as he traveled along the way, he touched on themes that he had been developing in his address to the gathering of scholars in Santa Barbara. In Calcutta, shortly after arriving in Asia, he spoke of the monk as being "a marginal person," explaining that the monk "withdraws deliberately to the margin of society with a view to deepening fundamental human experience." And with the Santa Barbara experience specifically in mind, he talked about "monks and hippies and poets," calling them "deliberately irrelevant."

> We live with an ingrained irrelevance which is proper to every human being. The marginal man accepts the basic irrelevance of the human condition, an irrelevance which is manifested above all by the fact of death. The marginal person, the monk, the displaced person, the prisoner, all these people live in the presence of death, which calls into question the meaning of life.

But, in the same address, he described how the margins can provide the appropriate circumstances for a resurgence of hope:

And so I stand among you as one who offers a small message of hope, that first, there are always people who dare to seek on the margin of society, who are not dependent on social acceptance, not dependent on social routine, and prefer a kind of free-floating existence under a state of risk. And among these people, if they are faithful to their own calling, to their own vocation, and to their own message from God, communication on the deepest level is possible.

He concluded this address by calling upon the same insights that was to inform his interpretation of the Buddhist sculptures at Polonnaruwa:

And the deepest level of communication is not communication, but communion. It is wordless. It is beyond words, and it is beyond speech, and it is beyond concept. Not that we discover a new unity. We discover an older unity. My dear brothers, we are already one. But we imagine that we are not. And what we have to recover is our original unity. What we have to be is what we are.[30]

His final address, on the morning of his death, offered vivid and explicit reference to his experience in Santa Barbara. It was a talk on "Marxism and Monastic Perspectives," and he prefaced it by describing the scene at the Center for the Study of Democratic Institutions where he had met young revolutionary leaders from all parts of the world.

He recalled that when he had introduced himself to one of the young leaders, he had been told, "But we are the true monks. You are not the true monks; we are the true monks." He had been pondering the statement, and he had come to some clarity on the matter:

> What does such a statement, such a suggestion, mean? What was he alluding to when he said that the revolutionary student is the "true monk," and the monk in the monastery is not a true monk? I think it gets around to one of the things that is most essential to the monastic vocation, which we have to some extent neglected.

And what has been neglected? What is essential to the true monastic vocation? On the day of his death, he summarized it this way:

> The monk is essentially someone who takes up a critical attitude toward the world and its structures, just as these students identify themselves essentially as people who have taken up a critical attitude toward the contemporary world and its structures. . . . In other words, the monk is somebody who says, in one way or another, that the claims of the world are fraudulent.[31]

In Santa Barbara, on October 3, he had said that one becomes a monk "to break through the inevitable artificiality of social life." But the thought was the same.

To the transcript of the dialogue that occurred at the Center for the Study of Democratic Institutions on that day, we have added two essays which Merton wrote expressly for the *Center Magazine*. Each deals with a theme that relates to the topic of his conversation. The one is an essay on "the city," and the second is an extended book review that delineates Merton's approach to "the wilderness." The two essays complement Merton's dialogue presentation.

In being able to produce (and reproduce) this material, I am grateful to Donald McDonald, recently retired director of the center and long-time editor of the *Center Magazine*, for the permission he has given and the assistance he has provided. Thanks, too, to Alan Brilliant and Unicorn Press. I also wish to thank M. Gerald Bradford, former administrative director of the center, for his assistance and encouragement.

It was a rich and energetic discussion that occurred in Santa Barbara on that Tuesday in October, now more than twenty years ago, and its significance has only increased as time has passed. We offer it here not only out of respect for the remarkable insight and uncommon wisdom of Thomas Merton but in tribute to the intellectual process that Robert Hutchins established.

WALTER H. CAPPS

THE CENTER
DIALOGUE

🌿 🌿 🌿

As was the custom at the Center for the Study of Democratic Institutions, Robert Hutchins, the president, opened each dialogue session with a background statement on the subject that was to be addressed. For this dialogue session, however, Hutchins called on W. H. "Ping" Ferry to frame the discussion topic and to introduce the guest of the day. The session followed an early-morning meeting with students on the subject of resistance to the Vietnam War, student protest, and cultural revolution. Merton had witnessed some of the meeting and had been talking informally with some of the participants. He had been telling them about his vocation, and they had been describing their own work in monastic terms. So they had been conversing about what it is to be a monk, how the true monk functions in the modern world (that is, within the turmoil of the world of 1968), and how authenticity in this respect is identified. "Who are the true monks?" they had asked. And this led to a

28

discussion of whether official, formal vows are necessary, and whether other persons, not officially identified in this way, may be carrying out fundamental monastic objectives. Merton was enjoying the conversation very much when Robert Hutchins pounded the gavel to announce the beginning of the next formal session. And, as we have noted, Hutchins turned to Ferry to begin the session.

Smiling broadly, as if poking fun at his distinguished guest, Ferry began by saying, "Right after I took Father Merton off the plane this morning, he handed me a book which had just been delivered to him. It is entitled *Zen and the Birds of Appetite* and is the most recent of his numerous books. The publisher is New Directions." But before Ferry could finish, Merton interjected, "this is a paid commercial." Following the laughter, Ferry continued: "I mention this book because it has to do with the topic that Father Merton will take up with us. By way of introduction, I want to read the first paragraph of the blurb," continuing the fun, "which is undoubtedly written by Tom himself." More laughter. "Thomas Merton is internationally recognized . . .'" Laughter. "Yes, it is written by Tom." More laughter. Ferry tried to continue, but Merton was wanting to interrupt. Ferry said: "Thomas Merton is internationally recognized as having one of those rare Western minds which is entirely at home in Asian experience." By now the room was quiet, as Ferry continued his recitation:

"In this collection of essays Merton writes about complex Asian concepts with a Western directness. One reason for this skill is that he has not only studied Buddhism from the outside, objectively, but has grasped it by empathy and living participation from within, while remaining a priest and Trappist monk." Ferry then called upon Merton to speak, and the dialogue is recorded as follows:

MERTON: Well, if ever anybody was put on the spot, I would like to know when it was. I have a feeling that I am about to go to Asia without having caught up on the amount of meditation I ought to do. [Merton explained that he had just returned from Alaska, where, he said, he had "been running around wildly."] What I want to do today is to give you some kind of account of the mischief I expect to get into in Asia. And then, with the hope that if I get back without dying of amoebic dysentery or other interesting things, I can give you an account, after the fact, of what happened when I got there. And I want to fit this into the context of what is known as monastic renewal. I can talk about this with complete equanimity here because I don't think there are any monks present—except, of course, the people who are the real modern monks, people who have taken over the function of monks in the modern world.

You hear this talk everywhere, or you hear it in monasteries, about monastic renewal, and it is confusing because, too often, it is employed to talk about the renewal of an institution. But as soon as people start talking in these terms, you can see that they are enveloped in what Sartre calls bad faith: If the life we are living is not meaningful in itself, how are we going to make an institution meaningful to other people? And what would be the point of making monasticism meaningful to other people? There is no point to this whatever.

So, what I am about to say has nothing to do with the meaningfulness of monasticism, or the meaningfulness of the monastic experience, or anything like this. It is my own personal, let's say, compulsion that drives me to Asia. I am out of the monastery for the first time in about twenty-five years, with the permission of a new abbot—who sort of fell out of the clouds, in a very providential way, into this position of authority. The old abbot, as Dr. Hutchins knows, was very strong on my not leaving the monastery, not going anywhere, or anybody going anywhere, and he became a hermit—which is what I've been too for the last ten years. And his [the new abbot's] first act was to attend Robert Kennedy's funeral, which got all of us off the hooks we were on about traveling.

So, what happened was that a meeting of abbots—of Christian abbots—was set up for Bangkok in December, and I was invited to it and accepted the invitation, with the permission of the abbot. And then other things began falling out of the clouds too. At the end of October I'm supposed to be a meeting in Darjeeling, which has the grandiose name of a "Summit Meeting of Religions." At this meeting will be present all kinds of people representing, say, Buddhism, Jainism, Hinduism, and the various religions of Asia. And it seems to me that, though it won't achieve any of the things that it is trying to achieve, it may produce something very interesting.

I think we are at a moment of critical importance in . . . [pause] Well, I won't call it the dialogue between East and West in religion, but we are at the point where the exchange between the Eastern and Western religious experience can be decisive.

Last year Dom Aelred Graham, who is going to bring out a book on the subject in about a month,[1] went over there with a friend called Harold Talbott,[2] a young fellow, who is still there. I'm going to meet Talbott, I'm in correspondence with him, and we're working together, and things are developing. Talbott has met the Dalai Lama and is now living near the monastic center where the Dalai Lama lives. The Dalai Lama has given him a cottage, a Tibetan cook, and a guru.[3] Talbott is learning the Tibetan language and is about ready to enter into a rather deep study of Tibetan Buddhism and the things that are related to it. And there is a very good chance of some communication taking place.

You know, of course, that the Tibetan Buddhist monks are in exile, and are all over the north of India now. They're in the Himalayas and in Nepal, in Sikkim and in Bhutan. They're around Darjeeling. Thus, everything that is best in Tibetan Buddhism is scattered around up there. And I hope to see as much of it as I possibly can and to stay with it as long as I can. The plan for now is that I have six months, but my abbot says, "As long as you come back to America sometime, it's O.K." And I hope to stay as long as I possibly can over there, to be in and out of India and Nepal, and so forth.

I believe a great deal can be done and learned at the present moment, and not at all in terms of an official dialogue. I am not going there as an official representative of anything. And I'm not "dialoguing" for the Catholic Church with Buddhism. I am not trying to reach some kind of an agreement as to what we can agree on together. There is really no problem here. There is no problem whatever about Catholicism and Buddhism because they are two entirely different entities. Buddhism is not a religion in our sense of the word; rather, it is a totally different approach to reality. It's a religious approach, if you like, but it is not a theological perspective—not a salvational thing, but a psychological thing. And it is perfectly possible, for a Catholic to . . . [pause], and I think Catholics should. I think if Catholics had a little more Zen they'd be a lot less ridiculous than they are in some of their actions and words and so forth. If Catholics had a little more Zen, there'd be a lot less trouble about, say, birth control, for example. But I do think that there are immense possibilities here in contact with Tibetan Buddhism, which has an esoteric tradition. I believe it is quite possible for a Catholic to enter into the esoteric traditions of Tibetan Buddhism. There doesn't seem to be any reason why not. I haven't discussed this with any church authorities, of course. I'll discuss it after the fact if I get initiated into some esoteric traditions. But there seems to be no reason why one shouldn't be doing this."

[At this point, Merton, while pondering his next thought, was interrupted by Rexford Tugwell, former Governor of Puerto Rico, and member of President Franklin Roosevelt's "brain trust."[4] Tugwell suggested that "they'll put you back in the monastery when you return." Merton responded as follows:]

Yes, if they can catch me. [laughter] But you see, when you talk about monasticism, as I was saying a minute ago, it's not a question at all of making an institution meaningful and relevant to the world. It is a question of renewing an age-old experience. The real essence of monasticism is the handing down from master to disciple of an uncommunicable experience. That is to say, an experience that cannot be communicated in terms of philosophy, that cannot be communicated in words. It can only be communicated on the deepest possible level. And this, it seems to me, with all due respect to everything else that's going on, this to me is the most important thing. This is the only thing in which I am really interested. There is nothing else that seems to me to have the same kind of primary importance. And I would say this because it is beyond the level—and, of course, the Jungians and others have sensed this—it is beyond the level of psychology. There is a deeper dimension than psychology. It is a theological dimension, if you admit that theology is something more than dogma, something more than doctrinal formulation about something ultimate. And this is what I hope I am going to get into.

I am going into this without plans; that is, it is completely unplanned. There have been no plans except plans that have been made by the people who are organizing the summit meeting. But plans seem to be making themselves on every side in a way that almost scares me. Just as I arrived here this morning, Ping [Ferry] had a pile of mail for me in which five or six extremely exciting new contacts were set up for me. And I have the feeling that I am going there—I don't want to sound kooky about it—but somewhat carried by a force which is something a little bit more than me. I do think that we have that feeling sometimes in life, however you wish to explain it without being silly about it. There is such a thing as that dimension of life, which is when life is "meaningful." To me this is meaningful dimension of life.

What is going to come out of this, I don't know. I don't threaten to write one book about it, or two books about it. I have a very serious reservation about writing any books at all about it. Conceivably, this might finish me as a writer, which would be a consummation most devoutly to be wished. This might be the last because, after all, there are things that one doesn't talk about. Maybe nothing will come out of it for anybody. But it seems to me that this is the way things should develop, that you should reach a point where you go into something completely unknown, completely new, and you don't know what's going to happen.

The program at present, according to such plans as I have, includes India on the 15th of October, a meeting in Darjeeling that I have been talking about in the week of the 20th . . . We're all going out, all of us, and representatives of the different religions will stand on a mountain and watch the sun rise on Kanchenjunga, October 22, with silent prayer. This will be very nice; we'll all enjoy it and so forth. But there is a tea plantation north of Darjeeling which is run by a Catholic who is supporting a Tibetan Buddhist monastery which is next door. I hope to live there for a while and visit the Tibetan Buddhist monastery and get in contact with these people. I hope, too, to meet the Dalai Lama early in November and then go where he may have ideas as to where I ought to go. I will go where he suggests. I have to be back in Thailand in early December for the meeting of Catholic abbots. I plan to get there a little early to speak to an English Buddhist monk in Bangkok, who will put me in contact with some people in the up-country monasteries in Thailand, which, I understand, are the best ones.

The only fear I have of that is that, perhaps, by that time, our war effort may have spread to that area. I hope not. But this is a possibility.

Well, if I can, I will get to these monasteries in the woods in Thailand. But I can's stay there very long because I have to go to Indonesia where we have a monastery of our order of Cistercian monks.[5] I have to preach a retreat there. Apparently, it is one of the best monasteries of the order. One of the other monks who has been there tells me that they are real monks, and they have no Western problems at all. They're just simply monks, and they just pray and meditate and do what monks do. And they are not hung up on any of the matters that tend to worry us so much. So this should be a nice experience. But Indonesia is unexplored territory as far as the question of spiritual experience goes, because this is a whole new situation. They do not have monks in Indonesia. They are not only Moslems but what goes on there goes on in small secret groups of people who maintain a pre-Muslim tradition which is Hindu-Buddhist. This I find extremely interesting. There is only one book about it that I know of, a book by Clifford Geertz on the religions of Java.[6] It is a very interesting book. I recommend it to anyone who might be curious about this sort of thing.

There is a very interesting development of the

Hindu tradition in Indonesia which has been kept on sort of a secret level. For example, I am to go to a town called Solok, in the middle of Java, and there I am to meet a lawyer. But this lawyer is in fact the head of one of the secret spiritual groups that functions in Indonesia. His role is to give spiritual direction to the people who come to him. And the basic idea is that the real dimension within which things are happening is a spiritual one, and there is a spiritual obligation to keep Java on a somewhat decent spiritual level. No promises are made about what will come of this, but they feel that there is something very important going on which the Indonesians are a part of by virtue of their meditation. So they meditate consistently and frequently, and understand it to be part of what they consider to be Java's mission to the world.

There are other groups like this in Java. There is, in fact, one group—which I don't expect to see because access is extremely difficult—that lives in the jungle, isolated from everyone else. And they will not let you come to them at all unless you are willing to take a several-days' trek barefoot through the jungle. (I'm not ready for several days through the jungles of Indonesia barefoot. Maybe after the Dalai Lama gets finished with me, I may be up to it, but right now I'm not.) Presumably, when you get there, there is something extremely secret and interesting going on. I hear that sometimes they send a man down to Jakarta; he comes out of the jungle and comes down to Jakarta and makes a contact in Jakarta. They have no radios— nothing like this. They have no news—nothing. But he goes down to Jakarta; he meets certain people that he has to meet and says, "I want to see so and so; I want to see this one." And he contacts these individuals, and says, "*You . . . you . . . you . . .* You come back to our place. You do this. You do this. You contact these people. You go to America," and so forth. It all sounds very interesting, very romantic. But I don't know if I will gain access to these people.

There is a very interesting Dutchman in Java now who has become an Indonesian citizen, and who is one of the best experts on the Javanese puppet play—an important part of Javanese life. He is also an expert on the Javanese dance. I hope to run into him, and to follow along with him into whatever areas he feels to be interesting there.

So these are just some of the possibilities that are going to open up on this trip, I hope. So after Indonesia I hope to go back to India to pursue anything interesting that may have opened up there. And then ultimately Japan and the Zen monasteries. There is a man in Tokyo who is concerned about Shingan Buddhism, which is different from Zen, and he, apparently, is a very interesting person.

So, perhaps, I may be with you again in a year, or two years, and give you a report on what this was all like. It may turn out that it was all nonsense, and it may turn out that it was all romance—all a dream and so forth. Or it may turn out that I have something very interesting to say. Or I may just avoid the whole issue and not say anything to anybody about anything. I don't know. But I felt that this was a good opportunity, and I thought you might be interested. Before I start out, I have taken the opportunity to share with you my hopes and aspirations. And if you have any questions, or anything you'd like to discuss, why, I would be glad to . . .

DONALD MCDONALD:[7] Would you say a little bit—I suppose there is much to say—about why you see the need for monastic renewal in your order particularly or in any order. Has there been a falling away from the ideal monastic life?

MERTON: Well, you actually could answer this by providing a whole development of the issue. Monasticism as an institution—which is not what I am particularly interested in—definitely needs renewal. When I entered Gethsemani twenty-five years ago, I entered an institutional situation that had been solidified in the seventeenth century. It was Trappist, and it was marked by very strict rules of silence and so forth. I am glad for it. I mean it was an experience that I wouldn't have changed for anything. But it was inhuman, and impossible, for a lot of people. There is no point in trying to carry on something like this. There is no point whatever in trying to bring in young people from America now—in this kind of thing—and making them live the kind of silent life that we lived, with sign language, no heat, and bad food. You know, in Lent you get up, you have no breakfast, and you go out and break rock on the back road like a convict. This is fine. It's a wonderful experience. I'm glad I went through it, but I wouldn't want to impose it on anybody else, because it's useless. It's arbitrary. It's a sort of *acte gratis* that Gide talks about, you know.[8] And if you want to do it on that kind of basis, you can do it. That's fine. But you don't want to get committed to this for life.

There were times when I was a novice, I would be sleeping in the downstairs dormitory, and there was a man up in the infirmary screaming his head off all night because he'd gone completely out of his mind. And they wouldn't let him go because his vows hadn't expired; he was under temporary vows and had two more years to go. So he had to stay. Well, this calls for renewal.

Of course, by now, we've had a certain amount of renewal. You get a decent breakfast; you can get cornflakes if you want them. The cornflakes are there, and you can pick them. And there's more milk and all. I'm allergic to milk products, but they give me eggs and fish. And there is a new liturgy, and there is more time for reading.

But what I am really interested in is recovering the depths of the purpose that you are in a monastery for. And it is not just a question of an office, or of prayer that is intelligible to everyone, or music that they like better, or more liveable quarters. It is the question of why one becomes a monk, what you become a monk for, and I say this without any qualification: it is an unconditional breaking through the limitations that are imposed by normal society. You become a completely marginal person in order to break through the inevitable artificiality of social life. Artificiality is inevitable. There is no condemnation of social life in saying that it has to be artificial; it is bound, to some extent, to be artificial. But, of course, the problem that you get into is that you get into another society that is equally artificial. And this is the trouble that is experienced by the Tibetan Buddhists. It is the trouble with the Zen Buddhists. They all find themselves in the same predicament.

By the way, one of the things that interests me most is findng out whether or not they have anticipated the trouble that they are going to get into. They are not yet in the same trouble that we are in. I refer specifically to the Zen people. D. T. Suzuki, the great teacher, said that he thought Zen, as they have known it culturally, is already finished, and that it would have to move into an altogether different dimension, which of course Zen ought to be able to do.[9] Zen should be the most unlimited and most uncircumscribed approach to one's experience in life. And if they are doing what they are supposed to do, they should be doing this. But you see, as soon as Zen gets into our country, for example, well, what do they bring in? They bring in all the useless trappings from Japan. Everything that is non-Zen gets hung on Zen, and people begin to think that this is Zen. So for Zen to make any kind of sense, I suppose, they are going to have to drop all of the sitting in the cross-legged posture and the gongs and what not. Zen is going to have to do without all of this. And I'm sure a lot of the monks are prepared to do this.

FRANK KELLY:[10] Father Merton, is there anything corresponding to a pentecostal movement among these Eastern groups?

MERTON: Among the Eastern groups, no, but among us, yes. As I see it, the Western monk is faced with a choice between certain scenarios (will you forgive me for using the language of Herman Kahn?). First of all, the scenario that we have rejected is the baroque one, the one that belongs to the post–council of Trent period, which is rigid, ritualistic, and legalistic. But the traditional Western one—the one I have been trying to teach in the novitiate for a long time—is very hard to get across. But there is also a pentecostal mode, though this is not the one that attracts me. It may have a certain validity, but it is not what I am particularly interested in. But a lot of our monasteries are going somewhat pentecostal; I'm referring to some of the Trappist monasteries.

For example, there is a small Trappist foundation, an experimental foundation—in Illinois, I think—where there is definite contact with the local Pentecostal minister.[11] And I think they've all undergone the laying on of hands, and they've all received the Spirit. The Pentecostal minister comes in for Sunday Mass with his wife, and they speak in tongues. To me this is sort of a byway; it is not exactly what I think they're there for. But for some of us, well, even in our monastery there has been a sort of small pentecostal splinter group. But you must understand that we are a large monastery. You see, in Catholicism there is a strong pentecostal movement emanating from Notre Dame, which is reaching various segments of Catholic life in this country. I would call it "modified pentecostal," and I suppose it has a certain value. But, personally, I think that pentecostalism doesn't fit well with monastic life. It may be good for people who are not locked up in a little group together. If they are going to be out working somewhere, and then they come together on Wednesday night to speak in tongues, this is fine. But if you are going to be speaking in tongues from morning to night in a small enclosure behind the wall, this could lead very rapidly to rather unfortunate circumstances.

KELLY: I have heard that there was a strong pentecostal movement in Indonesia. Is this true?

MERTON: That could be. That could very well be, because they might tend to be inclined that way. You see, the Indonesians are extremely mystical in the broadest sense of the word. There are emotional people. And the groups that I have been referring to, the ones that get together secretly, have ways of controlling and monitoring the emotions. The Indonesians seem most interested in developing what they call *raza*, which is a Hindu concept, but it has been taken over by them. And everything in Indonesian culture, in pre-Moslem Indonesian culture, is oriented toward the development of *raza*, which is a kind of spiritual integration and balance, in which you are not overwhelmed by emotional forces (whether pentecostal or not). The idea behind this—for example, the Wayang movement, which is the movement of the Indonesian puppet play and is so central in Indonesian culture—is the dramatization of *raza*. Have you ever seen these plays? Here you have the dramatization of stories based on the *Mahabhrarata*, the great Hindu epic,[12] which has been transmitted to Indonesia and adopted by the Indonesian people. And they are interminable; the puppet plays go on all night long. They're shadow plays, and one can see these shadow figures constantly in conflict.[13] You go to the puppet play, you arrive there at 8 o'clock at

night, and you are in there until 3 o'clock in the
morning, with the conflict still going on. There is
but one man who is operating it, and it is all on the
screen. He sings the epic as he maneuvers the
puppets. There are good guys and bad guys. The
good guys are the good emotions, and the bad guys
are the bad emotions, personified as gods, evils,
demons, and so forth. The purpose of the session is
to bring about a kind of Aristotelian catharsis: you
are supposed to come away from it completely
pacified, for you have attained *raza* again. You see,
you are back again in a state of complete tranquil-
ity, peace, and balance, and you are ready for
anything.

I suspect that one reason the Indonesians are so
strong on this is that, as you also know, they
occasionally go berserk. They simply go absolutely
mad. They've had revolutions and counter-
revolutions; they've experienced blood purges
within which there is a kind of national berserk
episode. They fear this. They know this about
themselves. If you know an Indonesian, I mean, a
fully developed Indonesian person, you feel as if
you are sitting in front of a package of dynamite.
They are beautiful people. They are fantastic people. And they are filled with this tremendous potential of energy which you feel could really explode.

I was talking to the Indonesian ambassador
about Bali, for example, which is part of the picture. Bali is the one place where the Moslems never

got in. They've completely retained the old pre-Moslem Hindu way of life. And the ambassador said, "Look, when you are in Java, fine. Deal with the spiritual masses. But when you get to Bali, just be a tourist. Don't mess with the Balinese, because what is going on there is really too explosive." What is going on in Bali is an intensely magical thing. And he told me that in Bali one would run into demons that one can't handle. And, of course, the Balinese are trying to regulate this. Their dances, their ceremonies, and their theater are all concerned about keeping the demons in the right place.

EDWARD CROWTHER:[14] Would you comment on the validity, as you see it, of the influence of a great deal of Eastern mysticism on what one might describe, perhaps, as a kind of "pop spirituality" here in the West. When you look around, you see all of the right elements: the fusion of a great deal of Eastern mysticism with orthodox Christian spirituality such as meditation, and it is given a transcendental quality. What do you think of its validity? Is it speaking to orthodox Christianity. Is it really possible or valid to translate Eastern experience into Western terms? I'd like to get your appraisal.

MERTON: I'm convinced that it is an absolutely valid expression of need. I do not think, though, that the methods of satisfying this religious need are adequate, but there is no question about it: it is an expression of the need. After all, we are living in a society that is absolutely sick. And one of the reasons why it is sick is that it's completely from the top of the head. It's completely cerebral. It has utterly neglected everything to do with the rest of the human being; the whole person is reduced to a very small part of who and what the person is. Now, the development of the hippie movement, combined with the use of drugs, combined with the growth of other spiritual movements, is an outcry of protest against this imbalance. And Christianity has connived with this, you see. The official Christianity has simply gone along with this, that is, with this kind of repressive, partial, and fragmented view of the human person. And now we just have to face the consequences. I mean, you know, guitar Masses aren't going to do it.

JOHN SEELEY:[15] But you are saying more than this, aren't you? When you analyze students you talk of their election to become marginal for the sake of becoming vocal, and you relate this to the original thrust of the monastic movement.

MERTON: Yes, exactly. The monastic movement is marginal in its denial of the thesis that society has the right answers. What is the origin of the Christian monastic movement? You recall that it is the Constantinian integration of Christianity into the

Roman Empire. At this precise point, people go out into the desert and say no. This is the basis for the sensitivity that the monk is not a priest.

Oh, yes, I should not be a priest. I didn't want to be a priest, but it was part of the system, so I became one. All right. No problem.

But the monk should not be a priest. The monk is a layperson in the desert, who is not incorporated into the hierarchy. The monk has nothing to do with an establishment. But of course as soon as the monk gets into the desert, he discovers a desert establishment, and there is the same problem. You know, in the lifetime of the originators, this problem had already arisen. It is a very interesting history. I've always had a temptation to try to write a history of the late fifth century in Alexandria. Athanasius used the monks, you see, in the struggle against the Aryans. The monks were stupid, so you just give them an orthodox doctrine and say, "Go to it boys. You are defenders of the faith!" But even here you will find intensely independent people. The more they get regimented into something, the more somebody breaks off and goes further away. And it seems to me that, perhaps, what I am doing in this breakthrough to Asia might be a sort of protest in reaction to the present situation within Christian monasticism in this country.

BISHOP JAMES PIKE:[16] Father Merton, your mention of the desert reminds me that in my ongoing avocation of studying Christian origins I have come to the conclusion, for the time being, that the Christian-Jewish movement is simply a continuation of activities that were transpiring within the desert, involving other groups—the Essenes, for example, a John the Baptist sect, and so forth. And it goes back to the age-old conflict between grazers and farmers, or between mobile people who travel light and more structured situations within the cities, with their institutions. Christianity, in its earliest form, is the heritage of the desert.

MERTON: Exactly. Absolutely. There is no question about this. This is tied up with the question of idolatry. The agrarian established civilization has its roots in the land and is tied up with a cycle—a fertility cycle of harvest, planting, and so forth. With this comes the fertility gods and the fertility cults, with fertility sacrifices . . . Well, the desert movement is a protest against this. It is an effort to break through the immobilization of life in a cycle. If you read Exodus and Deuteronomy in this light, you will find that what is behind the prohibition against idolatry is that one is not to be tied to the fields or even tied to the fertility cult. Instead, it is a sense of the presence of Yahweh with the people of God. It is mobile. It is wide open.

GERALD GOTTLIEB:[17] You understand that there is a relationship between idolatry and property, then?

MERTON: Yes, exactly. Of course, this is the great problem today. We are in the same kind of situation. With property you get an idolatrous cult of possession and efficiency, and this makes for profits. And pretty soon you have a man standing up and saying that he'll bomb Vietnam into the stone age. Strictly speaking, this is the Canaanite blood sacrifice all over again, and it is perfectly logical in this context.

SEELEY: I place the idolatry of our society, perhaps wrongly, somewhat deeper, that is, more generally than property. I see it as a deeper spirituality. What distinguishes us from the East, in my view, is that we share in the idolatry of control, taken in its larger meaning, of which property is only a small part.

MERTON: I would certainly agree.

GOTTLIEB: Both of those elements would relate to the agrarian development?

MERTON: Sure . . . You see, I am a firm believer in the neolithic civilization as the time when we were really civilized people. But I don't know if I dare to say things like this anymore, but anyway. It seems to me that for two thousand, maybe three thousand years, you had a culture, an agrarian culture, in which war was not yet terribly important. But with the building of the city, you get a new element. Here you get the tyrant, then you get his army, and then you get the accumulation of wealth, and then you get the lust for power and so forth. And if you notice in the Hebrew prophets, especially Amos, the harking back to the desert ideal is also an attack on the city. I think Howard [Lewis] Mumford understands this situation clearly and stated it accurately. Therefore, what happens is not only the development of an agrarian-fertility idolatry, but with it, the idolatry of the city, followed by the idolatry of the nation. In our time, the idolatry of the power of the nation is something that people find absolutely irresistible. Most people find it irresistible, I should say. Yes, even in Kentucky, where I come from, they find it irresistible.

Incidently, let me say that Kentucky is in a frightening state at the moment, everyone with George Wallace stickers on their bumpers. But what I noticed most about this summer in Kentucky was the large amount of noise everywhere, simply from people firing off guns at every moment of the damn night. A lake near where I've been living has become a kind of Coney Island for the local kids, and they spend their whole day shooting beer cans in the lake, or shooting at fish, or shooting at turtles. It is perpetual gunfire. Where they're getting the bullets, I don't know. They can't begin to afford the ammunition that they're using, which someone must be giving them.

And then about three weeks before I left, I was

having some friends up for a Sunday afternoon, at the hermitage. We were sitting out in front under the poplar tree. And it sounded like a war was going on out there on the road. I don't know what was happening. Apparently, about eighteen guys surrounded a cornfield and shot everything that came out, in dove season. They couldn't have spent the whole afternoon firing at that cornfield; I don't know what they were doing. I mean, there aren't that many doves in all of Kentucky. But the entire afternoon sounded like an army maneuver. It is a frightening atmosphere. But to get back to the main theme.

The question of idolatry is the big religious question. And it seems to me, where the churches have gotten themselves in trouble is that they haven't seen this issue. You see, the church simply proposes a different idol. "This one is a better one because it is a more spiritual one," or something like this. But we must get rid of the idols.

JUDY SALTZMAN:[18] Father, do you think that the political and religious rebellion of young people in the United States, especially the turning to the teachings of the Maharishi, or to the writings of Asian mystics, as well as the interest in Zen, might possibly tend to create a more serious interest among us? I find that a good many of my contemporaries seem to be interested in reading the Christian mystics, St. John of the Cross, for example. Would you find this turning away from traditional

Christianity toward the East responsible for an eventual turning back to a different form of Christianity, one that might even be more genuine?

MERTON: Yes, I think so. But I don't think Maharishi has got anything much. All he has is the most simple, obvious thing, a kind of quiet meditation practice, which is all right, but not worth all that much . . . What's that?

KELLY: Well, he's got an infectious giggle on television.

MERTON: Has he? I haven't seen that . . . But the thing that really makes me wonder a bit about the progressive Christians is their staunch repudiation of the mystical element in religion and their firm approbation of the nineteenth century, which is what they're trying to catch up with right now.

PETER MARIN:[19] The one thing that puzzles me is that, back at the beginning, you talked about the Zen discipline and sitting cross-legged, and you had some reservations about that. But what throws me is this: are you talking about a transformation of consciousness when you talk about religious sensibility?

MERTON: Sure.

MARIN: . . . without that kind of intense discipline, without the means of achieving a real transformation of consciousness, rather than just affecting attitudes?

MERTON: This is absolutely correct. There is no question about it. You do have to do something difficult, and you have to impose on yourself a discipline which lasts a long time. So when I was talking about sitting cross-legged, I wasn't repudiating discipline. I was simply saying, "Look out for the external forms. It is so easy to take the external forms for the reality."

MARIN: All right. But my next question is this? Traditionally those forms of discipline have been religious. But now there is a kind of secularization that goes on, and religious values are being carried over, more and more, into social areas by young people. Are there, in these areas, the means for the same kinds of discipline? Specifically, when young persons get involved in politics and social issues, while they are not being idolatrous, there tends to be a form of destruction that runs in the opposite direction from the rationale for the monastery. And I wonder if there is any mediation between the two kinds of concern.

MERTON: At present that really is a large problem, because what is going on in the radical side of

Christianity is a movement toward the revolutionary mystique as the only valid discipline. If you are
not committed to revolution, everything that you
say or do is irrelevant.

Now all of this is very fine. I'm not prepared to
say anything very much about this because I'm
worrying about it myself. I don't know. But I
wonder if Dan and Phil Berrigan, for example, are
. . . I wonder if that's the right track, you see? I
don't know. I suppose everybody wonders about
this. You've got to give them credit for having the
courage to opt for something, and they've gone
through with it, and this is fine. And I haven't . . .
you know. This is a great thing. But I wonder if it is
a blind alley. I refer to the form that it takes. Are
they just going to get themselves beaten over the
head until they're beaten to a pulp, and then what?

MARIN: My question was somewhat different. I am
not sure that revolutionary activity and monastic
living really do achieve the same objective. I'm not
willing to agree to that very easily.

MERTON: I don't think they do either, actually.
Personally, I am completely committed to one of
these. A revolutionary mystique, for me, would be a
complete illusion. I mean, this is irrelevant to me.
What I have to do is to examine this traditional
posture, because I happen to have an opening

toward it, and I happen to have the background to do it, and so forth. A man can only do one thing at a time. And this is the thing that I think that I should do.

JOHN WILKINSON:[20] Oh, I just wanted to ask a very simple question, Father. You described what seems to be universal human experience when talking, for example, about the shadow play, which, as you mentioned, exists in a vast form from China to Greece. Plato knew of it, of course. Its epicenter seems to be, if anywhere, the Turkic-speaking peoples. Anyway, is there any way in which you could say that there is a specifically Christian mysticism? I can understand the "fundamental humanity" part of it, but what is specifically Christian?

MERTON: Well, here you have run into the subject that Heiler took up in his book on prayer. I refer to the distinction between the mystical and the prophetic. If you want to be fussy about it, you can take the Christian and Jewish investment in prophetism and so forth and clearly distinguish this from universal religious experience. Now, whether this has to be done or not, I don't know. But if you want to be specific about it, I suppose that this is what you have to do. Personally, though, I'm much more interested in the universal, you see. The prophetic tradition is fine, for it moves into the revolutionary mystique much more easily.

Those who are devoted to the revolutionary mystique can point back to the prophets or to the apocalyptic sects of the late Middle Ages, to Joachim of Fiore. But I prefer to follow the other strand.

PIKE: This is a question I would have raised earlier, but I'm glad I didn't, because I'd rather raise it in this form precisely because I agree with you. I share with you the interest in the more universal approach. You know, I've been associated with Bishop John Robinson, the two of us now having accepted panentheism rather than dualism as a more plausible explanation of reality, and do not feel that this is contradictory to our Christian profession. But in doing this, I worry a little about something I've been talking to a few people about, Alan Watts and others. And I haven't found a satisfactory answer. The situation is that many of us in the West are oriented toward universal religious experience yet are engaged in social concerns of a rather prophetic posture. But what is the connection? What is the relationship between this universal sensibility and involvement in a social ethic in order to bring about change?

MERTON: That's a heck of a question. The thing that really obscures this for us is that the universal perspective tends to get tied up with a static social structure; hence, as soon as you start to talk about it, you're hung up with a vision of a static past that extends over thousands of years in which nothing ever happens. Now, the idea of the prophetic word breaking through this tends to become associated with the idea of revolution and change. By now we are all conditioned, whether we know it or not, to think in terms of prophecy, revolution, on the one side, and this quiet mystical type of religion, with a static society, on the other. This is one of the puzzles I'm trying to figure out. This is one of the reasons I'm going to the East, to find out about this.

SEELEY: But isn't it possible that the question is wrongly, in fact, idolatrously, posed, as though there could be but a single answer. And is it not likely that whatever answer one gets would be the same kind of answer that the few studies on creativity have shown us, namely, that it consists, insofar as we know anything about it, in a capacity to erect immense and rigorous structures, together with a capacity to allow these to dissolve into an unformed flow and flux, out of which a new structure which embodies something more arises.

MERTON: The great thing would be to place it in a different context. We've got to see it differently.

REX TUGWELL: Are you going to be greatly disappointed if you find the Asians very much institution-oriented, that is, very much interest in politics?

MERTON: I expect them to be, in many ways.

TUGWELL: They seem to be from here.

MERTON: I don't know what I'm going to run into. The Dalai Lama may be running a kind of crypto-fascist operation. I don't know. Anything is possible.

TUGWELL: Well, let us hear from you, will you?

MERTON: When I get back, we'll . . .

GOTTLIEB: Father, do you associate the following concepts together: expiation, guilt, mortification of the flesh, limitation of the mind, idolatry, fanaticism?

MERTON: Umhm.

GOTTLIEB: The reason I raise this . . . well, it is not the product of thought, but rather a matter of feeling on my part. I've always felt that there is a close relationship between the concepts of mortification and the concepts of idolatry, and that both of them are essentially antireligious, in the sense of being an abnegation of human existence.

MERTON: Well, yes. This fits into what we've been saying about power. When you get the idea of power invested in a repressive authority, a father figure of some sort, then I suppose it all boils down to what Freud was talking about . . . you know, a kind of extension of the castration bit all the way down the line.

And I know that certainly in Trappist life, that's what a lot of it amounted to. It would be very interesting to write the book that one could really write about a Trappist monastery. I don't think I'd ever be able to get away with it. I mean, this whole idea of power invested in a paternal type of authority, who, in various sorts of ways, is constantly cutting down the kids, you see, cutting down the sons and holding things back . . . What comes clear is the futility and stupidity and triviality of this view of life, you see. Now this is restricting life to a ludicrous limit, in which illusion is perpetuated, and the real thing is not eliminating certain pleasures or eliminating certain fulfillments but eliminating illusion. The first illusion that has to be eliminated is this dualistic illusion of power and subjection. This is the enemy. This is what we have to fight.

MARIN: I want to go back to another question, one that is still floating about. I refer to the distinction, which I think is artificial, between the internal and the external. This is obviously a mistaken way of seeing it, and yet it is very difficult to get out of it. But what happens is that one tends to think of a kind of internal liberation as opposed to some kind of external social activity of liberation. Obviously, the two seem to occur simultaneously, though not always. But I ask this because the impulse in social activity is to create a kind of community, which is ultimately supportive in the same way that I think religion has traditionally been supportive. The point at which you can afford to let structures collapse is the point at which you have an internal relation to something other than the structure. So my real question—but I realize that it is probably silly to ask this of any particular person—is whether it is possible to create a community which is not, by its very nature, idolatrous. That is, to the extent the community is supportive, one is bound to support the community. How then do persons build up relationships other than within the community? I understand the impulse toward religion, but I have not in practice or in activity really found, within those terms, a building up of the kind of support, or of a degree of sureness in relation to the world, that I'm talking about.

MERTON: This is something that I really don't know. I can't say. Professionally and vocationally, I know the hermit line, you see. And this implies a basic distrust of community—I mean, community in any organized sense. Can there be a community that will fulfill, say, the requirements of community in the Bible? I hope so. I don't know. Mystically, I believe so. Eschatologically, it's got to happen. But I've never seen much indication of it.

But don't tell anybody that I said this! I'm a member of the Roman Catholic Church in good standing. It is supposed to be the Catholic Church that is doing this. But as I say, the evidence is, well, you've got to take it on faith.

CROWTHER: I wonder how long it is going to be before the eruptive quality of the many exciting facts of the spirituality of the so-called underground church are going completely to make redundant the extremely dull facets of the established spirituality within the institutional church?

MERTON: I don't know. Your guess is as good as mine on that.

CROWTHER: I mean, I find as a bishop of the church that the church is a colossal, smacking great bore, don't you?

MERTON: Yes.

CROWTHER: Well now, when you and I agree that we both find church a crashing bore, well, what does the poor guy in the pew think? You know, I suffer. I bleed with him.

PIKE: They don't think it is a bore. That's the problem.

KELLY: No, many of them don't.

CROWTHER: Well, they're the ones who go to our services.

MERTON: Do they think it, or are they just telling themselves this? This is what bothers me about the people who are so enthusiastic over—see, I have just come from Alaska, where I have witnessed a great argument between conservatives and progressives—playing guitars and singing a new type of hymn. This was regarded as relevant. Are they kidding themselves or what?

CROWTHER: It's sugar on the old pill, isn't it?

MERTON: Sure.

KELLY: I think the danger, though, with bishops and other professionals in the field of religion is they do get bored because they see the machinery going around, whereas the layperson is free to ignore the machinery and concentrate on the experience.

PIKE: But the press has spoiled this; ever since the encyclical *Humanae Vitae* no laypersons could ignore the machinery.

KELLY: Many do. You'd be surprised how many just pay no attention to it.

CROWTHER: Well, with a name like Kelly, you can say this.

WILLIAM GORMAN:[21] There is a certain pattern in this discussion about the possibility of genuine community, and it refers back to an earlier comment of yours that the young revolutionaries are the monks of the modern world. And yet this analogy isn't yet very substantial.

MERTON: No.

GORMAN: The monk as being deliberately marginal and committed for the purposes of individual and personal experience to marginal existence—is this consistent with the notion that you are not going to reform society because the real community is the mystical community? If you are going to destroy the existing society in order to produce one that is genuinely characterized by human relations that do add up to community and love and so on, couldn't you rightly be charged with some "holy confusion" on this point?

MERTON: You're correct on this.

GORMAN: Not all can be monks. Here would be an obvious logical contradiction: nobody would be marginal if everyone were a monk. So there will be cities of one size or another. They will have as part of their intention to achieve, through the building of community, the greatest possible sustenance for a good human life. This is the purpose of communities regardless of the fact that they might be in terrible shape and vulnerable to all kinds of fantastic charges. In my view, this is still what they're trying to do.

But what I am leading up to is this, that there is a kind of secular philosophical implication of the doctrine of original sin that has become part of the Western intellectual tradition. And it may be that, in reflecting on the experience of the fact that community, in this mystical sense, has never been achieved, and in committing yourself to the hermit life, you have already decided, so to speak, that its chances are not very good. I'm simply reflecting on the revolutionary mystique that develops around social action in search of unattainable ideals in the world, and I am just square enough to still have a dualism of two cities. I have colleagues here who believe that Augustine's *City of God* was one of the most damaging things that happened to the human race. But I'm not of this opinion. It could be that some old-fashioned, square version of this secular interpretation, or secular explication of the implications of original sin, is a salutary part of human wisdom for terrestrial existence. And this old-fashioned idea may have some purpose to play against the excesses of the revolutionary mystique. Would you go along with any part of what I've said?

MERTON: Well, sure. This was perfectly true of the twelfth century.

FERRY: We've often pointed this out to Bill.

GORMAN: I have my own fashion of being marginal, and it's chronological.

MERTON: I'm not only agreeing with you, but I'm saying that the twelfth century worked. It could work then because there weren't so many people, and it was a workable situation. But when you look at our time, and at what is going on today, well, I don't know. What is happening today is an unprecedented kind of explosion.

GORMAN: All right. I enjoyed your answer, and I even plead guilty to being a chronological-type monk, if you like. But I was trying to offer some wisdom about the limitations of achievement in terrestrial existence as being intrinsic to human life as a piece of twentieth-century wisdom that is badly needed. I say this because I see young people of high spiritual quality who are committed to a kind of mystique about the revolution, and to my mind, the revolution has a good chance of becoming an idol. Even in the church, the current renewal is being directed, more and more, to the social order and to the conviction that the testimony of the love of God is to achieve something by way of reform in the order of justice. Now, I'm not against justice. I'm just urging that there are some limitations to the achievement of it that are probably intrinsic. In addition, the transformation of the love of God into love of community, even when it is done badly, is not much good for the world. I'd call it a large new heresy. And, along the way, I'm for burning heretics, too.

JOHN COGLEY:[22] I wish to add to what Bill has said and to affirm it. It would seem to me that his insight into the human condition is also descriptive of monasticism or anything else. You always come up against original sin, and you can't get away from it even in Trappist Kentucky.

MERTON: There is more of it there than most places.

SALTZMAN: I'd still like to go back to Peter Marin's comment concerning internal and external relationships. And I'd like to hear one more comment on the problem that faces many young people today, the choice between a kind of religious mysticism within which consciousness is changed and the choice of social action. After all, how can you lead a revolution if you are the same kind of little person that may have led the revolution in 1789? And yet, I find this a terribly difficult choice to make, because it places one in a dichotomy. And yet, you are a man who has taken up a social position, and yet you have remained apart from the world. Perhaps you can't answer this, but how do you remain involved and detached at the same time? I think this is the question that many of us are facing.

MERTON: Well, it is a problem for me too. Perhaps I can sum up some thoughts about solitude and society, or solitude and community, by saying that the important thing is that, however you look at it, we are not going to solve social problems, or the problems of community, unless we solve them in universal terms. Today it is a question of getting everybody to be able to see things in some way that is communicable among all of them. There has to be one world in which we all experience our problems as common and solve them as common without repudiating individual national differences.

The task of the solitary person and the hermit is to realize within himself, in a very special way, a universal consciousness and to contribute this, to feed this back insofar as he can, into the communal consciousness which is necessarily more involved in localized consciousness, and in such a way that there will be a kind of dialectical development toward a more universal consciousness. At the moment, I think this is highly possible. However you wish to approach it, we are moving today toward the possibility of more and more real communication. But it has to be real communication, and not just American funnies in India. There is where it starts to come together. I see my particular aspect of it in terms of the spiritual and the personal. But I know that I have to be aware of these other problems, and I make whatever commitment I can make on this, without getting into somebody else's job. But I think we must all get to the point of being universal persons. And in whatever way we go about it, we're not going to solve our problems unless we are all more and more thoroughly universal, and this is catholic, in that sense of the word, catholic people.

FERRY: I think this is a very uplifting note on which to conclude this session. Thank you very much, Tom.

THE SACRED CITY[1]

❧ ❧ ❧

Thomas Merton

Today the Valley of Oaxaca is one of the poorest and least productive areas of Mexico. It was once one of the richest and most fertile. It was also the home of Monte Alban, probably the first real city on this continent. What was this city? What kind of culture flourished there? What kind of people lived there?

Recent archaeological studies have brought to light some very detailed material concerning the Zapotecan culture of the Oaxaca Valley. We are finally in a position to fit Monte Alban into the general picture of Mesoamerican civilization of the "classic" age, before the rise of the Mixtecs, Toltecs, and Aztecs, whose culture was essentially decadent.

Before we even begin to speak of Monte Alban and of the ancient Mayan cities which had much in common with it, we should put out of mind the generalized notion of ancient cities associated with Egypt and Mesopotamia or our sketchy knowledge of postclassic Mexican (Toltec and Aztec) culture in the five centuries preceding the Spanish conquest. In these ancient cultures the city stands out as the stronghold of a monarch or tyrant, a potential empire-builder with an army and a culture based upon slavery. The city, in other words, comes into being with kingship, or at least with militaristic autocracy; urban culture is not only commercial but above all militaristic. True, the less well-known archaic cultures of the Cretans and Etruscans seem to have been less warlike, but they were also more isolated.

The popular view of Mexican and Mayan culture, based primarily on the reports of the Spanish conquerors, gives us an idea of a colorful but bloodthirsty and necrophilic city life in which war, slavery, and human sacrifice play a dominant part.[2] In a word, when we think of the first cities we instinctively think also of war, power, wealth, autocracy, empire, and so on. Possible exceptions (such as Jerusalem, the "City of Peace") are too ambivalent to be exceptions. But the first cities in America were not like Nineveh, Babylon, Ur, or Thebes—or Rome. The Western "ideal" city has always been Athens the independent, the democratic, the sophisticated. Could Monte Alban or Tikal be compared with Athens? Not really, except in so far as they were highly aesthetic cultures and seem to have been in a certain sense "democratic," though perhaps not in a way that fits our present concepts.

The most recent studies of Mesoamerican culture enable us to reconstruct a general picture of man and civilization on our continent, and in order to situate Monte Alban correctly it might be well to look first at the general picture.

We now know that hunters of mammoth were established in the Valley of Mexico as far back as 12,000 B.C., when the continental ice sheet came as far south as the Ohio River and Mexico had a cool, rainy climate. With the extinction of the big game a new kind of culture developed. Agriculture seems to have been introduced after 7000 B.C. with the rudimentary cultivation of squash and then eventually of maize.

Where was maize first grown? For a long time the highlands of Guatemala were thought to be the place where corn was originally cultivated. Recently, discoveries in a dry area of northern Oaxaca have given us a complete sequence of ancient remains of maize in its evolution from a wild to a domesticated plant. This domestication certainly goes back beyond 4000 B.C. At any rate, for a thousand years or more a neolithic, maize-growing, seminomad, preceramic culture flourished in Mexico. Ceramics began to be made around 3000 B.C. but never entirely supplanted stone implements, which continued in use down to the Spanish conquest. Thus we have some two millenia and more of neolithic village life before the appearance of a city in Mexico.

How did the Mesoamerican city develop? It was not primarily the result of a population explosion. The first city, rather, developed as a cult center. There is evidence of such centers among the Olmecs in the jungle lowlands of Vera Cruz. Many of the Mayan cities were merely centers for worship, sometimes uninhabited except by a small population of priests and scholars who were occupied with determining the proper dates for clearing, planting, etc., and the lucky or unlucky days for various activities.

For an authentic urban center, a moderate concentration of population and of economic activity is required, as well as a development of science that includes the knowledge of writing and of chronology—and of course astronomy and mathematics. One also seeks evidence of planning and of monumental public buildings: in other words, evidence of a relatively advanced culture which both stimulated and satisfied the aesthetic and intellectual needs of the community. This appeared in Monte Alban several hundred years before the construction of the Maya cities of Guatemala.

The city of Monte Alban was built somewhere between 1000 and 500 B.C. by Zapotecan Indians who knew writing, had a calendar, were astronomers, and were probably the first urban dwellers in America. Pottery findings at Monte Alban have brought to light examples of a style that goes back to about 800 B.C. But with the paving of the Great Plaza after 300 B.C. the classic period of urban culture at Monte Alban was definitely established.

There is a certain amount of complexity in the terms used by scholars, due to the fact that the word "classic" has become ambiguous. Until recently it was assumed that the Mexican and Mayan urban cultures were all roughly contemporaneous, and "classic" was used loosely to describe any urban culture. Attempts to find a more accurate classification have resulted in complex charts and correlations, with preclassic, classic, and postclassic or epiclassic broken up into numerous subdivisions, and reaching out to include the widely different cultures of Guatemala, Yucatan, Vera Cruz, Mexico, Oaxaca, etc. These charts may be very illuminating to the experts, but to the generalist they are not much help.

To put it in the simplest terms we can lump together everything from 1000 B.C. to 900 A.D. as "classic" or "early" (though it includes various degrees of preclassic and late classic). This is a convenient and clear division because about 900 A.D. Monte Alban was abandoned and so were the "classic" Maya cities like Peten, Uaxactun, and other centers in Guatemala. After this time, the Mayan culture spread out in Yucatan in a postclassic civilization under Toltec domination.

In the Oaxaca Valley the old Zapotec society yielded to Mixtec conquerors, who occupied fortified towns of the region like Mitla and Yagul.

The six-hundred-year period between 900 A.D. and the Spanish conquest can be called "postclassical" or "late." By the time the Spaniards arrived, even the last, postclassic Mayan cities of Yucatan had been abandoned. Mayan urban civilization was at an end. But Aztecs had a flourishing city of 300,000 people at Tenochtitlan (the site of Mexico City).

There were great differences between the two cultures and the two periods. In the early cultures there is almost no evidence of militarism, of war, or of human sacrifice until very late. The late civilization resulted from the radical change from a peaceful to a warlike and militaristic way of life brought in by conquering tribes from the north. The Mixtecs conquered the Zapotecs, who had abandoned Monte Alban (though still sporadically worshiping there). The Toltecs overcame the Mayas and produced a hybrid Toltec-Mayan culture in Yucatan, centered especially in Chichen Itza. It is with the "late" period that history really began.

In the classic period there were no chronicles. Even though there were many dated stelae in classic Mayan architecture and at Monte Alban, the "dates" were at first nonhistorical. They referred to cosmic cycles, to the stars, and to events that may be called "divine" rather than historical. In other

words, the classic chronologists were more concerned with cosmic happenings than with the rise
and fall of empires, with gods rather than kings.
Not that this concern with the gods excluded care
for human existence. By liturgy and celebration,
the lives of men, cultivators of maize, were integrated in the cosmic movements of the stars, the
planets, the skies, the winds and weather, the
comings and goings of gods.

That this society was not dominated by what
Marx called religious alienation is evident from the
fact that its art did not represent the gods until
very late: the early art represented the people
themselves, the celebrants officiating in liturgical
rites and feasts, vested in the splendid and symbolic emblems of their totem.

We are only just beginning to realize the extraordinary sophistication of totemic thought (as inter-
preted by Claude Levi-Strauss). Living records left
by such North American Indians as Black Elk and
Two Leggings suggest that the elaborate symbolic
association of the human person with cosmic
animals represents something much more intimate
than an "alienated" subjection to external forces.
We know something of the profoundly interior
relationship of the North American hunter with his
"vision person," and we know that the Central
American Indian remained in extremely close relationship with the divinity that ruled the day of his
birth and gave him one of his names. What we have

here, then, is in fact not an example of alienation but of identity, but obviously a conception of identity quite different from our subjective and psychological one. It was, however, centered on the ego.

This "objective" identity seems to have been fully integrated into a cosmic system which was at once perfectly sacred and perfectly worldly. There is no question that the Indian in the "sacred city" felt himself completely at home in his world and understood his place in it perfectly. And this is what we are to understand, apparently, from the splendor and symbolism of an art which signified that the gods were present not in idols or sanctuaries so much as in the worshiper, in his community, and in his world. The individual found himself, by his "objective" identity, at the intersection of culture and nature, crossroads established by the gods, points of communication not only between the visible and the invisible, the obvious and the unexplained, the higher and lower, the strong and the helpless, but above all between complementary opposites that balanced and fulfilled each other (fire-water, heat-cold, rain-earth, light-dark, life-death).

"Self-realization" in such a context implied not so much the ego-consciousness of the isolated subject in the face of a multitude of objects as the awareness of a network of relationships in which one had a place in the mesh. One's identity was the intersection of cords where one "belonged." The intersection was to be sought in terms of a kind of musical or aesthetic and scientific synchrony—one fell in step with the dance of the universe, the liturgy of the stars.

What kind of life was led in the "classic" cities of Guatemala or Oaxaca? We can say that for roughly two thousand years the Zapotecan and Mayan Indians maintained an entirely peaceful, prosperous civilization essentially aesthetic and religious. This civilization was focused in urban cult-centers, but it was not what we would call a truly urban culture.

Although it has been maintained that Tikal once had a population of 100,000, the Maya cities were usually quite small, with few permanent residents apart from the priests and scholars who served the temples and observatories. Most of the population was more or less rural, living outside amid the cornfields, which were periodically cleared from the jungle and then allowed to run wild again.

Since there was no war, at least on any scale larger than perhaps family or tribal feuding, there was no need to concentrate the population within fortified towns—until, of course, the postclassical period. It was perfectly safe for families, clans, and other small groups to live in jungle villages as they had done from time immemorial.

The city was where they came together for special celebration, for the worship that included the games and the dances that gave them intense satisfaction and a heightened awareness of themselves. This worship was also completely integrated in their seasonal round of clearing the milpa, burning brush, planting, cultivating, and harvesting the maize. It did not take up an exorbitant amount of time. In periods of enthusiasm and prosperity the people gave their surplus time and energy to the common construction projects that some modern scholars still find hard to understand. The example of Egypt and Assyria would suggest slave labor, yet all the evidence seems to indicate that the Mayans and Zapotecans build their classic cities spontaneously, freely, as a communal expression of solidarity, self-awareness, and aesthetic and religious creativity. There is no evidence of slavery until the postclassical period.

The success of these two thousand years of peaceful, creative existence demanded a well-developed sense of coordination, a division of tasks under the direction of specialists, a relatively high proportion of skilled labor, and above all a unanimous acceptance of a common vision and attitude toward life. One must, of course, avoid idealizing what was still in many respects a Stone Age culture, but one cannot evade the conviction that they must have been very happy people.

The Mayan scholar Sylvanus Morley quotes an English statesman who said: "The measure of civilization is the extent of man's obedience to the unenforceable." Morely comments that by this standard the Mayans measured high. John Paddock, writing of the Zapotecs of Monte Alban, remarked that there is no evidence of slavery there: "No whipcracking slave driver was needed. The satisfaction of helping to create something simultaneously imposing, reassuring and beautiful is enough to mobilize endless amounts of human effort."

Paddock went on to argue from the persistence of pilgrimage and generosity in the Mexican Indian of today: "It is common for tens of thousands of men, women and children to walk fifty or more miles to a shrine. They are not slaves: they would revolt if denied the right to make their pilgrimage. . . . Mexico's shrines of today are in most cases far less beautiful and the worshiper's participation (with money) is far less satisfyingly direct; but they still come by the thousands voluntarily."

What Paddock was trying to explain is not merely the fact that a "sacred city" like Monte Alban existed, but that it was in fact built on a mountain ridge, without the use of wheels for transport, without draft animals—and also without slave labor. The fantastically difficult work was carried out with immense patience and love by people whose motives cannot even be guessed if we try to analyze them in economic or technological terms.

Here was a major religious capital, an urban complex which at the height of its prosperity "occupied not only the top of a large mountain but the tops and sides of a whole range of high hills adjoining, a total of some fifteen square miles of urban construction" (Paddock). The maintenance of the city "would necessarily require the services of thousands of specialists: priests, artists, architects, the apprentices of all these and many kinds of workmen, including servants for the dignitaries and their families."

The peaceful and continuous growth of this city and its culture—with continued renewal of buildings and art work century after century—can only be explained by the fact that the people liked it that way. They wanted to build new temples and to dance in the Great Plaza dressed in their beautiful costumes. Nor were they particularly anxious to find quicker and more efficient methods of doing their work. They were in no hurry. An artist was content to grind for months on a jade pebble to carve out a glyph, and he was not even paid for it! As Paddock wrote,

> In purely economic terms, in fact, the whole accomplishment seems fantastic. But if we attempt to comprehend it in economic terms alone we are neglecting the crucial factors. For over a century we have been living in a world where technology has been the great hope, solving one problem after another. Perhaps we may be forgiven if we have come to demand material-mechanical explanations for everything, overlooking the possibility that they

may often be insufficient. . . . To ask these
questions only in economic, technological or
political terms will produce only some of the
needed answers. Questions about religion and
art must be included, and they may be in this
case the most basic ones.

The chief economic factor in the success of the
Zapotec civilization was that in the fertile, isolated
Oaxaca Valley a relatively small population, which
remained stable, had a highly effective system for
exploiting the natural advantages of their region.
They could produce the food they needed—plenty
of corn, squash, tomatoes, peppers, avocados, red
and black beans, cacao, along with tobacco and
cotton. They engaged in some commerce with the
so-called "Olmec" civilization in the jungle lowlands of what is now the State of Vera Cruz, and
later with the people in the Valley of Mexico to the
north. But their surplus time and energy went into
art, architecture, and worship.

The result was a city and culture of great majesty
and refinement, integrated into a natural setting of
extraordinary beauty, dominating the fertile valley
surrounded by high mountains. The people who
collaborated in the work and worship of the sacred
city must have enjoyed a most unusual sense of
communal identity and achievement. Wherever
they looked, they found nothing to equal their
creative success, which antedated that of the
classic Mayan culture by more than five hundred

years and was not eclipsed by the latter when it finally came into being.

The archaeology of the Oaxaca Valley is still in its first stages; further discoveries will bring to light much more that has been barely guessed at so far. But we know enough to surmise accurately what it was all about. Paddock said:

> Monte Alban was a place electric with the presence of the gods. These gods were the very forces of nature with which peasants are respectfully intimate. . . .
>
> Every temple stood over half a dozen temples of centuries before. Buried in the great temples were ancient high priests of legendary powers, now semi-deified; centuries of accumulated wealth in offerings, centuries of mana in ceremonies, centuries of power and success, lay deep inside that masonry. But with their own humble hands, or those of their remembered ancestors, the common people had made the buildings. . . . They were participating in the life of the metropolis; they could see that they were making it possible. They could stand dazzled before those mighty temples, stroll half an hour to circle the immense open plaza, watch the stunning pageantry of the ceremonies, stare as fascinated as we at the valley spread out mile after mile below. They knew that no other such center existed for hundreds of miles—and even then their city had only rivals, not superiors.

Three things above all distinguish this "sacred city" from our own culture today: indifference to technological progress, a lack of history, and the almost total neglect of the arts of war. The three go together and are rooted in a conception of man and of life entirely different from ours.

It is a difference between a peaceful, timeless life lived in the stability of a continually renewed present and a dynamic, aggressive life aimed at the future. We are more and more acutely conscious of traveling, of going somewhere, of heading for some ultimate goal. They were conscious of having arrived, of being at the heart of things. Mircea Eliade speaks of the archaic concept or the sanctuary as the axis mundi, the center or navel of the earth, for those whose lives revolve in the cycles of its liturgy.

Perhaps the inhabitants of these first American cities, who remained content in large measure with Stone Age technics and had no sense of history—certainly no foresight into what was to come after their time—simply accepted themselves as having more or less unconsciously achieved the kind of successful balance that humanity had been striving for, slowly and organically, over ten thousand and more years. Their material needs were satisfied and their life could expand in creative self-expression. This was the final perfection of the long, relatively peaceful agrarian society that had grown out of the neolithic age.

According to our way of thinking, the Zapotecs were crazy not to make use of the wheel when they knew of its existence. The curious thing is that they actually had wheels but used them only for toys. They did use rollers to move heavy blocks of stone. They were perfectly capable of "inventing the wheel" but for some reason (which must remain to us profoundly mysterious) never bothered. They were not in the least interested in going places.

The Indian cultures of Mesoamerica are typical archaic societies in which the creative energy of the people found expression in artistic and religious forms rather than in applied science. This is, to us, one of the most baffling of problems. Greco-Roman civilization—which was much more pragmatic and practical than that of the Indians—also presents this problem. The science of the Alexandrian scholars in the Roman Empire was sufficiently advanced to permit the development of steam engines. The industrial revolution might have but did not take place in 200 A.D. So might the discovery of America for that matter: The Alexandrian geographers were aware that the earth was round.

What is most perplexing to us is that, as a matter of fact, economic conditions called for this kind of development. To our way of thinking, the Zapotecs needed wheels and machinery, and the economy of the late Roman Empire demanded a technological revolution. Just as the Mesoamerican Indians used wheels only for toys, so the Romans used hydraulic power only for shifting heavy scenery in the Circus.

A few modern scholars have tried to grapple with this enigma. Hanns Sachs, a psychoanalyst, contends that the urge for technological progress was suppressed in the ancient world because of the radically different disposition of narcissism and libido in ancient man. Tools and machines replace the body and absorb or alienate libido energy, which is frankly cathected by sensuous man.

Once again we come upon the curious question of archaic man's sense of identity. His sense of his own reality and actuality was much more frankly bound up with sensual experience and body narcissism. We, on the contrary, have been split up and tend to project our libido outward into works, possessions, implements, money, etc. In the lovely sculptured "danzantes" of Monte Alban, with their frank and sensuously flowering male nakedness, we apprehend a bodily awareness that substantiates what Sachs says:

> To these men of antiquity the body, which they could cathect with a libido still undeviated, was their real being. . . . Animistic man vitalized the inanimate world with such narcissism as he could find no other use for.

The "reality" and "identity" of archaic man was, then, centered in sensuous self-awareness and identification with a close, ever-present, and keenly sensed world of nature; for us, our "self" tends to be "realized" in a much more shadowy, abstract, mental world, or indeed in a very abstract and spiritualized world of "soul." We are disembodied minds seeking to bridge the gap between mind and body and return to ourselves through the mediation of things, commodities, products, and implements. We reinforce our sense of reality by acting on the external world to get ever-new results. Primitive man did not understand this; he recoiled from it, striving to influence external reality by magic and self-identification.

The primitive, like the child, remained in direct contact with what was outside him; he was most happy when this contact was celebrated in an aesthetic and ritual joy. He related to the things and persons around him with narcissistic play. Our narcissism has been increasingly invested, through intellectual operations, in money, the machine, and weaponry; they are the extensions of ourselves, which we venerate in our rituals of work, war, domination, and brute power.

Obviously the Zapotecs of Monte Alban knew what violence was. They knew what it meant to fight and kill: they were not a "pacifist society" (which would imply a conscious and programmatic refusal of war). They just had no use for war. It was pointless. They were not threatened, and it evidently did not enter their heads to threaten others— until the far end of the classic period when a growing population had exhausted the reserves of lands, the deforested mountains were eroded, and the hungry community began to look for places to plant corn in the territory of others, or to fight others who came looking for more room in Oaxaca.

By this time, of course, the long centuries of high classic civilization were coming to an end everywhere in Mexico and Yucatan. Already in the seventh century A.D. the metropolis of the Valley of Mexico, Teotihuacan, had been sacked and burned. In the tenth century Monte Alban, was deserted. But it was never conquered and indeed never attacked. There were never any fortifications, and indeed there was never any need for any. There is no evidence of violent, revolutionary destruction—the city was not harmed. It just came to an end. The enterprise of sacred culture closed down. Its creativity was exhausted.

There is no satisfactory explanation yet as to why the classic sacred cities of the Mayans and Zapotecs were simply abandoned. Presumably the ancient civilization finally grew too rigid and died of sclerosis. Its creative and self-renewing power finally gave out. Sometimes it is assumed that the people became disillusioned with the ruling caste of priests and revolted against them. But we also hear of a migration of priests and scholars into the south, under pressure of invasion from the north. In any case the cities were abandoned.

The Zapotecs were conquered by their neighbors the Mixtecs after Monte Alban was abandoned, but they continued to live under their conquerors, maintaining, it is said, a government-in-exile somewhere else. Today, the Zapotecs persist, their language is still spoken, and in their ancestral territory they have outlasted the Mixtecs, who remain in a minority.

The Spanish conquered Mesoamerica in the sixteenth century. The blood-thirsty Aztec empire, built on military power, ruled Mexico. But it was hated and decadent. It was willingly betrayed by other Indians and collapsed before the guns of Christian Spain. Much of the ancient Indian culture was destroyed, and, above all, anything that had to do with religion. But the finest Mesoamerican civilizations had already disappeared seven or eight hundred years before the arrival of the Europeans.

After the conquest, the Oaxaca Valley, once rich and fertile, gradually became a near-desert as the ancient agricultural practices were forgotten and the soil of the deforested mountains washed out. Contact with the Europeans was in many ways a human disaster for the Mexicans. The Indian population of Mesoamerica was probably 20 million in 1519. In 1532 it was already under 17 million; in 1550 it was down to 6 million; and in 1600 there were only a million Indians left. The population dropped by 19 million in eighty years. This was due to diseases that the Indians could not resist. The impact of Spain on Mexico, then, was genocidal. Fortunately, a slow recovery began in the mid-seventeenth century.

The extraordinary thing about the Zapotec civilization of the Oaxaca Valley, above all, is that it maintained itself without military power for many

two thousand warless years of Monte Alban into our own world view. It may help to tone down a little of our aggressive, self-complacent superiority, and puncture some of our more disastrous myths. The greatest of these is doubtless that we are the first civilization that has appeared on the face of the earth (Greece was all right in so far as it foreshadowed the United States). And the corollary to this is that all other civilizations, and particularly those of "colored" races, were always quaintly inferior. We are far too convinced of many other myths about peace and war, about time and history, about the inherent purpose of civilization, of science, of technology, and of social life itself, and these illusions do us no good. They might be partly corrected by a sober view of the undoubted success achieved by the Zapotec Indians.

The "sacred cities" of Monte Alban and of Guatemala, as we see them, looked back rather than forward. They were the fulfillment of a long development of a certain type of agrarian culture that flourished in small populations. With the growth of populous societies, the accumulation of wealth, the development of complex political and religious establishments, and above all the expansion of invention and resources for war, human life on earth was revolutionized. That revolution began with what we call "history." It has reached its climax now in another and far greater revolution which may, in one way or other, bring us to the end of history.

Will we reach that end in cataclysmic destruction or—as others affably promise—in a "new tribalism," a submersion of history in the vast and unified complex of mass-mediated relationships which will make the entire world one homogeneous city? Will this be the purely secular, technological city, in which all relationships will be cultural and nature will have been absorbed in technics? Will this usher in the millennium? Or will it be nothing more than the laborious institution of a new kind of jungle, the electronic labyrinth, in which tribes will hunt heads among the aerials and fire escapes until somehow an eschatological culture of peace emerges somewhere in the structure of artifice, abstraction, and violence that has become man's second nature?

THE WILD PLACES[1]

✿ ✿ ✿

Thomas Merton

Man is a creature of ambiguity. His salvation and his sanity depend on his ability to harmonize the deep conflicts in his thought, his emotions, his personal mythology. Honesty and authenticity do not depend on complete freedom from contradictions—such freedom is impossible—but on recognizing our self-contradictions and not masking them with bad faith. The conflicts in individuals are not entirely of their own making. On the contrary, many of them are imposed, ready made, by an ambivalent culture. This poses a very special problem, because he who accepts the ambiguities of his culture without protest and without criticism is rewarded with a sense of security and moral justification. A certain kind of unanimity satisfies our emotions and easily substitutes for truth. We are content to think like the others, and in order to protect our common psychic security we readily become blind to the contradictions—or even the lies—that we have all decided to accept as "plain truth."

One of the more familiar ambiguities in the American mind operates in our frontier mythology, which has grown in power in proportion as we have ceased to be a frontier or even a rural people. The pioneer, the frontier culture hero, is a product of the wilderness. But at the same time he is a destroyer of the wilderness. His success as pioneer depends on his ability to fight the wilderness and win. Victory consists in reducing the wilderness to something else, a farm, a village, a road, a canal, a railway, a mine, a factory, a city—and finally an urban nation. A recent study, *Wilderness and the American Mind*[2] by Roderick Nash is an important addition to an already significant body of literature about this subject. It traces the evolution of the wilderness idea from the first Puritan settlers via Thoreau and Muir to the modern ecologists and preservationists—and to their opponents in big business and politics. The really crucial issues of the present moment in ecology are barely touched. The author is concerned with the wilderness idea and with the "irony of pioneering, [which was] that success necessarily involved the destruction of the primitive setting that made the pioneer possible."

Mr. Nash does not develop the tragic implications of this inner contradiction, but he states them clearly enough for us to recognize their symptomatic importance. We all proclaim our love and respect for wild nature, and in the same breath we confess our firm attachment to values that inexorably demand the destruction of the last remnant of wildness. But when people like Rachel Carson try to suggest that our capacity to poison the nature around us is some indication of a sickness in ourselves, we dismiss them as fanatics.

One of the interesting things about this ambivalence toward nature is that it is rooted in our biblical, Judeo-Christian tradition. We might remark at once that it is neither genuinely biblical nor Jewish nor Christian. Mr. Nash is perhaps a little one-sided in his analysis here. But a certain kind of Christian culture has clearly resulted in a manichean hostility toward created nature. This, of course, we all know well enough. (The word "manichean" has become a cliche of reproof like "Communist" or "racist.") But the very ones who use the cliche most may be the ones who are still unknowingly tainted, on a deep level, with what they condemn. I say on a deep level, an unconscious level. For there is a certain popular, superficial, and one-sided "Christian worldliness" that is, in its hidden implications, profoundly destructive of nature and of "God's good creation" even while it claims to love and extol them.

The Puritans inherited a half-conscious bias against the realm of nature, and the Bible gave them plenty of texts that justified what Mr. Nash calls a "tradition of repugnance" for nature in the wild. In fact, they were able to regard the "hideous and desolate wilderness" of America as though it were filled with conscious malevolence against them. They hated it as a person, an extension of the Evil One, the Enemy opposed to the spread of the Kingdom of God. And the wild Indian who dwelt in the wilderness was also associated with evil. The wilderness itself was the domain of moral wickedness. It favored spontaneity—therefore sin. The groves (like those condemned in the Bible) suggested wanton and licentious rites to imaginations haunted by repressed drives. To fight the wilderness was not only necessary for physical survival, it was above all a moral and Christian imperative. Victory over the wilderness was an ascetic triumph over the forces of impulse and of lawless appetite. How could one be content to leave any part of nature just as it was, since nature was "fallen" and "corrupt"? The elementary Christian duty of the Puritan settler was to combat, reduce, destroy, and transform the wilderness. This was "God's work." The Puritan, and after him the pioneer, had an opportunity to prove his worth—or indeed his salvation and election—by the single-minded zeal with which he carried on this obsessive crusade against wildness. His reward was prosperity, real estate, money, and ultimately the peaceful "order" of civil and urban life. In a seventeenth-century Puritan book with an intriguing title, Johnson's *Wonder Working Providence* ("The Great Society"?), we read that it was Jesus Himself, working through the Puritans, who "turned one of the most hideous, boundless and unknown wildernesses in the world . . . to a well-ordered Commonwealth."

Max Weber and others have long since helped us recognize the influence of the Puritan ethos on the growth of capitalism. This is one more example. American capitalist culture is firmly rooted in a secularized Christian myth and mystique of struggle with nature. The basic article of faith in this mystique is that you prove your worth by overcoming and dominating the natural world. You justify your existence and you attain bliss (temporal, eternal, or both) by transforming nature into wealth. This is not only good but self-evident. Until transformed, nature is useless and absurd. Anyone who refuses to see this or acquiesces in it is some kind of half-wit—or, worse, a rebel, an anarchist, a prophet of apocalyptic disorders.

Let us immediately admit that superimposed on this is another mystique: a mystique of America the beautiful—America whose mountains are bigger and better than those of Switzerland; scenic America which is to be seen first, last, and always in preference to foreign parts; America which must be kept lovely, for Lady Bird. (So don't throw that beer can in the river, even though the water is polluted with all kinds of industrial waste. Business can mess up nature, but not you, Jack!) This mystique—this cult of nature—took shape in the nineteenth century.

The romantic love of wild American nature began in the cities and was an import from Europe. It had a profound effect on American civilization. Not only did poets like William Cullen Bryant proclaim that the "groves were God's first temples," and not only did the nineteenth-century landscape painters make America realize that the woods and mountains were worth looking at; not only did Fenimore Cooper revive the ideal of the Noble Primitive who grew up in the "honesty of the woods" and was better than city people; but also it was now the villain in the story (perhaps a city slicker) who ravished the forest and callously misused the good things of nature.

The Transcendentalists, above all, reversed the Puritan prejudice against nature, and began to teach that in the forests and mountains God was nearer than in the cities. The silence of the woods whispered, to the man who listened, a message of sanity and healing. While the Puritans had assumed that man, being evil, would only revert to the most corrupt condition in the wilderness, the Transcendentalists held that since he was naturally good, and the cities corrupted his goodness, he needed contact with nature in order to recover his true self.

All this quickly turned into cliche. Nevertheless, the prophetic work of Henry Thoreau went deeper than a mere surface enthusiasm for scenery and fresh air. It is true that Walden was not too far from Concord and was hardly a wilderness even in those days. But Thoreau did build himself a house in the woods and did live at peace with the wild things around the pond. He also proved what he set out to prove: that one could not only survive outside the perimeter of town or farm life but live better and happier there. On the other hand, having explored the Maine woods, he had enough experience of the real wilds to recognize that life there could be savage and dehumanizing. Hence he produced a philosophy of balance which, he thought, was right and necessary for America. He already saw that American capitalism was set on a course that would ultimately ravage all wild nature on the continent—perhaps even in the world—and he warned that some wilderness must be preserved. If it were not, man would destroy himself in destroying nature.

Thoreau realized that civilization was necessary and right, but he believed that an element of wildness was a necessary component in civilized life itself. The American still had a priceless advantage over the European. He could "combine the hardiness of the Indian with the intellectualness of civilized man." For that reason, Thoreau added, "I would not have every part of a man cultivated." To try to subject everything in man to rational and conscious control would be to warp, diminish, and barbarize him. So, too, the reduction of all nature to use for profit would end in the dehumanization of man. The passion and savagery that the Puritan had projected onto nature turned out to be within man himself. And when man turned the green forests into asphalt jungles the price he paid was that they were precisely that: jungles. The savagery of urban man, untempered by wilderness discipline, was savagery for its own sake.

It has been consistently proved true that what early nature philosophers like Thoreau said, in terms that seemed merely poetic or sentimental, turned out to have realistic and practical implications. Soon a few people began to realize the bad effects of deforestation. As early as 1864 the crucial importance of the Adirondack woods for New York's water supply was recognized. About this time, too, the movement to set up National Parks was begun, though not always for the right reasons. The arguments for and against Yellowstone Park (1872) are instructive. First of all, the area was "no use for business anyway." And then the geysers, hot springs, and other "decorations" were helpful manifestations of scientific truth. Then, of course, the place would provide "a great breathing place for the national lungs." Against this, one representative advanced a typical argument: "I cannot understand the sentiment which favors the retention of a few buffaloes to the development of mining interests amounting to millions of dollars."

John Muir is the great name in the history of American wilderness preservation. Muir's Scotch Calvinist father was the kind of man who believed that only a sinner or a slacker would approach the wilderness without taking an axe to it. To leave wild nature unattacked or unexploited was, in his eyes, not only foolish but morally reprehensible. It is curious, incidentally, that this attitude has been associated rather consistently with the American myth of virility. To be in the wilderness without fighting it, or at least without killing the animals in it, is regarded as a feminine trait. When a dam was about to be built in a canyon in Yosemite Park in 1913 to provide additional water for San Francisco, those who opposed it were called "short haired women and long haired men." Theodore Roosevelt, though a friend of John Muir, associated camping and hunting in the wilds with his virility cult, and this has remained a constant in the American mystique.

Muir traveled on foot through a thousand miles of wild country from Indiana to the Gulf of Mexico. The reason he gave for the journey was that "there is a love of wild nature in everybody, an ancient mother love, showing itself whether recognized or no, and however covered by cares and duties." This was not mere regression, but a recognition of the profoundly ambiguous imbalance in the American mind. Muir saw intuitively that the aggressive, compulsive attitude of the American male toward nature reflected not strength but insecurity and fear. The American cult of success implied a morbid fear of failure and resulted in an overkill mentality so costly not only to nature but to every real or imaginary competitor. A psychological study of John Muir would reveal some very salutary information for modern America.

An investigation of the wilderness mystique and of the contrary mystique of exploitation and power reveals the tragic depth of the conflict that now exists in the American mind. The ideal of freedom and creativity that has been celebrated with such optimism and self-assurance runs the risk of being turned completely inside out if the natural ecological balance, on which it depends for its vitality, is destroyed. Take away the space, the freshness, the rich spontaneity of a wildly flourishing nature, and what will become of the creative pioneer mystique? A pioneer in a suburb is a sick man tormenting himself with projects of virile conquest. In a ghetto he is a policeman shooting every black man who gives him a dirty look. Obviously, the frontier is a thing of the past, the bison has vanished, and only by some miracle have a few Indians managed to survive. There are still some forests and wilderness areas, but we are firmly established as an urban culture. Nevertheless, the problem of ecology exists in a most acute form. The danger of fallout and atomic waste is only one of the more spectacular ones.

Much of the stupendous ecological damage that has been done in the last fifty years is completely irreversible. Industry and the military, especially in America, are firmly set on policies that make further damage inevitable. There are plenty of people who are aware of the need for "something to be done"; but consider the enormous struggle that has to be waged, for instance in eastern Kentucky, to keep mining interests from completing the ruin of an area that is already a ghastly monument to human greed. When flash floods pull down the side of a mountain and drown a dozen wretched little towns in mud, everyone will agree that it's too bad the strip-miners peeled off the tops of the mountains with bulldozers. But when a choice has to be made, it is almost invariably made in the way that brings a quick return on somebody's investment—and a permanent disaster for everybody else.

Aldo Leopold, a follower of Muir and one of the great preservationists, understood that the erosion of American land was only part of a more drastic erosion of American freedom—of which it was a symptom. If "freedom" means purely and simply an uncontrolled power to make money in every possible way, regardless of consequences, then freedom becomes synonymous with ruthless, mindless exploitation. Aldo Leopold saw the connection and expressed it in the quiet language of ecology: "Is it not a bit beside the point to be so solicitous about preserving American institutions without giving so much as a thought to preserving the environment which produced them and which may now be one of the effective means of keeping them alive?"

Leopold brought into clear focus one of the most important moral discoveries of our time. This can be called the ecological conscience, which is centered in an awareness of man's true place as a dependent member of the biotic community. The tragedy that has been revealed in the ecological shambles created by business and war is a tragedy of ambivalence, aggression, and fear cloaked in virtuous ideas and justified by pseudo-Christian cliches. Or rather a tragedy of pseudo-creativity deeply impregnated with hatred, megalomania, and the need for domination. Its psychological root doubtless lies in the profound dehumanization and alienation of modern Western man, who has gradually come to mistake the artificial value of inert objects and abstractions (goods, money, property) for the power of life itself. Against this ethic Aldo Leopold laid down a basic principle of the ecological conscience: "A thing is right when it tends to preserve the integrity, stability, and beauty of the biotic community. It is wrong when it tends otherwise."

In the light of this principle, an examination of our social, economic, and political history in the last hundred years would be a moral nightmare, redeemed only by a few gestures of good will on the part of those who obscurely realize that there is a problem. Yet compared to the magnitude of the problem, their efforts are at best pitiful; and what is more, the same gestures are made with great earnestness by the very people who continue to ravage, destroy, and pollute the country. They honor the wilderness myth while they proceed to destroy nature.

Can Aldo Leopold's ecological conscience become effective in America today? The ecological conscience is also essentially a peace-making conscience. A country that seems to be more and more oriented to permanent hot or cold war making does not give much promise of developing either one. But perhaps the very character of the war in Vietnam—with crop poisoning, the defoliation of forest trees, the incineration of villages and their inhabitants with napalm—presents a stark enough example to remind us of this most urgent moral need.

Meanwhile some of us are wearing the little yellow and red button "Celebrate Life!" and bearing witness as best we can to these tidings.

NOTES

INTRODUCTION

1. Thomas Merton, *Zen and the Birds of Appetite* (New York: New Directions, 1968).

2. Some of these letters have been published in William H. Shannon, ed., *Thomas Merton: The Hidden Ground of Love* (New York: Farrar, Straus & Giroux, 1985), pp. 201–45.

3. Ferry was vice-president of the Center for the Study of Democratic Institutions from 1954 to 1969. Victor Navasky offered a profile of Ferry in "The Happy Heretic," in *Atlantic Monthly*, July 1966.

4. Thomas Merton, *The Asian Journal of Thomas Merton*, ed. Naomi Burton, Brother Patrick Hart, and James Laughlin (New York: New Directions, 1973).

5. Dietrich Bonhoeffer, *Letters and Papers from Prison*, ed. Eberhard Bethge (New York: Macmillan, 1953). I have explored similarities between Bonhoeffer's and Merton's cultural roles in my book *The Monastic Impulse* (New York: Crossroad, 1983). Merton has commented extensively on Bonhoeffer in *Conjectures of a Guilty Bystander* (Garden City, N.Y.: Doubleday, 1966).

6. Merton, "A Letter to Pablo Antonio Caudra Concerning Giants," in *Emblems of a Season of Fury* (New York: New Directions, 1963), pp. 70–87. Pablo Antonio Caudra is one of three Nicaraguan poets whom Merton especially liked, the others being Ernesto Cardenal and Alfonso Cortes.

7. Ibid., p. 78.

8. Ibid.

9. Ibid., p. 82.

10. Ibid., p. 81.

11. Ibid.

12. Ibid.

13. Ibid., p. 86.

14. Merton, *Mystics and Zen Masters* (New York: Farrar, Straus & Giroux, 1966).

15. Ibid., p. ix.
16. Ibid.
17. Ibid.
18. Ibid.
19. Merton, *Zen and the Birds of Appetite*, pp. 3–4.
20. Ibid., p. 4. Here Merton paraphrases Suzuki's description of Zen as presented in the latter's *The Essence of Buddhism* (London, 1946).
21. Ibid., p. 10.
22. Ibid., p. 12.
23. Ibid.
24. Ibid., p. 13.
25. Ibid.
26. Ibid., p. 22.
27. Ibid., p. 31.
28. *The Asian Journal*, pp. 233–34.
29. Cf. Walter Capps, *The Monastic Impulse*.
30. "Thomas Merton's View of Monasticism," in *The Asian Journal*, pp. 305–8.
31. "Marxism and Monastic Perspectives," in *The Asian Journal*, pp. 326–43.

THE CENTER DIALOGUE

1. Dom Aelred Graham is perhaps best known for his book *Zen Catholicism* (New York: Harcourt, Brace and World, 1963), a book which Merton read and consulted frequently. However, the book that Merton carried with him to Asia was Graham's *Conversations: Christian and Buddhist* (New York: Harcourt, Brace and World, 1968). And the book Merton was awaiting was Graham's *The End of Religion: Autobiographical Explorations* (New York: Harcourt, Brace and World, 1968).
2. Merton refers to Talbott frequently in *The Asian Journal*. Talbott had been confirmed at Gethsemani after becoming a Roman Catholic at Harvard in 1959. Subsequently, under the direction of Dom Aelred Graham, he journeyed to India, then studied under the Dalai Lama. It was Talbott who urged Merton to meet the Dalai Lama and who arranged the meeting. Both before and after the meeting, Merton traveled extensively with Talbott in northern India.

3. The monastic center is located near Dharamsala, in which city the Dalai Lama provided Talbott with a bungalow.

4. Rexford Tugwell, former governor of Puerto Rico, was a fellow at the center and was studiously at work drafting a proposed new constitution for the United States.

5. The Cistercian monastery in Java is called Rawa Senang, meaning "peaceful swamp."

6. Clifford Geertz, *The Religion of Java* (New York: Free Press, 1960).

7. Donald McDonald, former dean of the School of Journalism at Marquette University, was managing editor of the *Center Magazine* when this dialogue took place in 1968. He subsequently became editor and retired as acting director of the center in 1987.

8. Merton studied the writings of Gide, shortly after his father's death, when a student at Oakham School, in the county of Rutland, in England. He frequently mentions Gide, Huxley, and Hemingway together. He studied all three at the same time, and their influence was enduring.

9. Daisetz T. Suzuki, with whom Merton carried on extensive correspondence over the years, was very much in Merton's mind as he prepared to travel to Asia. He was planning to meet Suzuki in Japan at the end of the journey, prior to his return to the United States. Merton's book *Zen and the Birds of Appetite* includes a dialogue with Suzuki, "Wisdom in Emptiness," pp. 99–139.

10. Frank K. Kelly was a speech writer for President Truman, then served as an officer of the Fund for the Republic, the institutional sponsor of the project called the Center for the Study of Democratic Institutions. Kelly is author of *The Court of Reason: Robert Hutchins and the Fund for the Republic* (New York: Free Press, 1981).

11. I have it on good authority that the "small Trappist foundation" to which Merton refers here was one of a number of such temporary and informal organizations which sprang up during the post–Vatican II era. The same authority attest that the experiment, greeted with enthusiasm by some of the monks in the beginning, lasted for no more than several months.

12. The epic *Mahabharata*, which comes from the classic age of Hinduism, can be compared to the *Iliad*. It is the story about

great conflict between two peoples, the Kauravas and the Pandavas, resulting in victory for the Pandavas. The section of the *Mahabharata* known as the *Bhagavad Gita,* or "Song of the Lord," is the best known and loved Hindu scripture. As Merton's comments illustrate, the *Mahabharata* is familiar to all Hindus and to peoples in many other portions of Asia as well.

13. The *wayang purwa* is very popular in Javanese puppet theater. In it the Indian epics *Ramayana* and *Mahabharata,* in which the relationship between a deposed deity (Semar) and his sons (Garent and Petruk) forms the plot, are enacted. For a description of the workings of Javanese puppet theater, see Edward C. Van Ness, *Javanese Wayang Kulit* (Oxford: Oxford University Press, 1980).

14. C. Edward Crowther, an Episcopal bishop, came to the center from England, and with extensive experience in South Africa. He participated actively in center projects dealing with civil rights, developments in third world countries, and, of course, with the volatile situation in Africa.

15. John Seeley had taught sociology at the University of Chicago and had had appointments in psychiatry and political economy at the University of Toronto, York University, and at Brandeis before coming to the center. At the time of this dialogue, Seeley served as dean of the academic program at the center.

16. James Pike, former Bishop of the Episcopal Diocese of California, joined the center staff in 1966. In this discussion with Merton about the origins of Christianity, he is drawing upon reflections and ruminations subsequently made explicit in two books issued by his wife. See Diane Kennedy Pike, *Search: The Personal Story of a Wilderness Journey* (New York: Doubleday, 1970), and Diane Kennedy Pike and R. Scott Kennedy, *The Wilderness Revolt: A New View of the Life and Death of Jesus Based on Ideas and Notes of the Late Bishop James A. Pike* (New York: Doubleday, 1972).

17. Gerald Gottlieb was a consultant to the center who had suggested the formation of a Court of Man, which Frank Kelly describes as "a world tribunal with power to render judgments on those who misused authority" (*The Court of Reason,* p. 6).

18. Judy Saltzman, at the time of this dialogue, was a junior fellow at the center. She has since become professor of philoso-

phy at California State Polytechnic University in San Luis Obispo.

19. Peter Marin, at the time of this dialogue, was a fellow of the center, with primary responsibility for the fields of education and contemporary social and cultural change. He has since written extensively and perceptively on the situation of Vietnam War veterans, the homeless population, and on other disenfranchised and underrepresented groups.

20. John Wilkinson, at the time of the dialogue, was both fellow at the center and associate professor in the Department of Philosophy at the University of California, Santa Barbara. He is known, too, for his highly regarded translation of Jacques Ellul's *The Technological Society*.

21. William Gorman, a philosopher and expert in medieval intellectual history, also worked on various projects associated with the *Encyclopedia Britannica* during his long and distinguished tenure with the center.

22. John Cogley, who was religion editor of the *New York Times* before coming to the Center, was both fellow and editor of the *Center Magazine* at the time of this dialogue. As illustrated in this discussion, he frequently "got in the last word."

THE SACRED CITY

1. This essay first appeared in the *Center Magazine* 1, no. 3 (March 1968): 73–77. Merton describes it as "essentially an appreciation of a new collection of studies-reports on 'Discoveries in Mexican Archeology and History,' edited by John Paddock, under the title *Ancient Oaxaca*, and published by Stanford University Press in 1966." He adds that the book contains two very important surveys, 'Mesoamerica Before the Toltecs' by Wigberto Jiminez Moreno, and 'Oaxaza in Ancient Mesoamerica' by John Paddock. Eight other short papers by archeologists Alfonso Caso, Ignacia Bernal, and other scholars are mainly concerned with the relations of the Zapotec and Mixtec cultures after the 'classic' period. The two longer studies are essential for contemporary evaluation of Zapotec culture in its relation to the other civilizations of Middle America." Merton then makes reference to another source, Sylvanus Morley, *The Ancient Maya* (Palo Alto: Stanford University Press, 1956).

2. Merton notes that the same attitude is reflected in Jonathan Norton Leonard, *Ancient America* (New York: Time-Life Books, 1967).

THE WILD PLACES

1. This essay first appeared in the *Center Magazine* 1, no. 5 (July 1968): 40–45.

2. Roderick Nash, *Wilderness and the American Mind* (New Haven: Yale University Press, 1967). Mr. Nash is currently professor of history at the University of California, Santa Barbara.

DATE DUE			

Merton   220059